Think Like the Greats:

Lessons from History's Top Performers, Champions, and Masters

By Peter Hollins,
Author and Researcher at
<u>petehollins.com</u>

Table of Contents

Introduction

"Every achievement, big or small, begins in your mind."

- **Mary Kay Ash**

What makes a high achiever? The obvious answer is: achievement.

However, if you really think about it, you'll agree that high achievers have the same character before they achieve their goals as they do afterwards. By the same token, we can often recognize a high achiever even when they occasionally fail to achieve a particular goal.

This tells us that achievement is an external sign of something deeper–a characteristic mindset that predicts and enable success.

This may not seem like an important distinction to make, but if we wish to achieve our own goals in life, we need to consciously shift our focus. Rather than "I want to achieve," we might say, "I want to be the kind of person that achieves."

In the modern world, we have a limited idea of what it means to be accomplished. We may get distracted by external manifestations–the perfectly executed piano recital, sports game, or speech–while failing to appreciate the state of mind required to bring those actions about. As a consequence, we may be tempted to mimic the *behavior* of people we consider successful, without appreciating the source of that behavior.

This is where this book comes in. Fortunately for us, history is filled with high achievers of all kinds; they hail from different time periods and backgrounds, have worked in different fields and areas, and have lived out stories of contribution and excellence that are totally distinct and unique. And yet, in the chapters that follow, you'll see that high achievers tend to be startlingly alike in their basic mindset.

How did these historical high achievers *think*? How did they understand their problems and challenges? What beliefs and assumptions shaped their inner lives?

The people we discuss in this book were certainly blessed with certain talents, aptitudes, and intellectual gifts, but this is *not* what makes them special. In these pages you won't find stories of easy genius or effortless victories. Instead, you'll see that high achievers are consistently those who are willing to work much, much harder than others, and often in unconventional and inspired ways. It is not that they were masterful in a specific area, but rather that they have mastered the art of excellence itself and applied it to their chosen area.

Chances are you're not a Nobel prize-winning scientist or a world-renowned philosopher, but whoever you are and whatever the size of your ambitions, the right attitude can help you achieve at the very limit of your potential–and expand that potential.

As you read, you'll be prompted to contemplate and actively apply some of the key concepts to your own life. Of course, no self-help book can tell you what precise shifts of belief and attitude will be most beneficial for you, but rest assured that with a little conscious reflection on your part, you can uncover these insights yourself. Keep focused and stay accountable to yourself. Work hard. Remember that mediocre attitudes produce mediocre results, and that a good idea only has value once translated into action in the real world.

As Mary Kay Ash noted, achievement begins in the mind–but that's not where it ends! The right attitude is the seed, your consistent and disciplined action is what grows that seed, day after day. Achievement is the fruit.

Let's dive in and take a look at how this eternal story has played out again and again in the lives of some of history's most prominent high achievers.

Marcus Aurelius

"Waste no more time arguing what a good man should be. Be one."

> -   **Marcus Aurelius**

We will begin our journey with Rome's second-century philosopher-emperor Marcus Aurelius, who not only led a nation but maintained a deep commitment to personal wisdom and ethical leadership. Despite facing wars, plagues, and political betrayals, he governed with remarkable equilibrium. Inspired by the prevailing Stoic philosophy of the time, his personal writings in *Meditations*–never intended for publication–reveal a leader wrestling with power, mortality, and the challenge of maintaining virtue in a chaotic world.

His reign marked the end of the "Five Good Emperors" era and left a legacy of leadership through philosophical wisdom. *Meditations* still tops bestseller charts, and Aurelius' writings re-capture the interest of every new generation. Today, Aurelius is cherished as an accessible source of timeless Stoic wisdom, while his reign as emperor receives relatively less airtime. We can see in his continued appeal a deeper truth: **Aurelius was a "high achiever" not because of his political acumen or leadership, but because of his mastery of *self-governance*.**

It's hard to imagine now, but in the time of Aurelius, kings, emperors, and heads of state were expected to oversee not just the judicial, military, and economic wellbeing of their nations, but their metaphysical and moral development, too. Thus, a good emperor would need to understand questions like, what is a human being? What is a *good* human being? How ought a good human being live? An honorable and rightful emperor, then, ruled from the wisdom acquired in correctly answering these questions.

Aurelius' sentiments are a reflection of broader Stoic ideals: accepting what you cannot control and focusing on developing inner virtue to live a meaningful life, regardless of external circumstances. For the ancient Romans, Stoic philosophy provided a practical framework for the formation of a virtuous life; such a life did not depend on fleeting pleasures like wealth or status, nor was it threatened by equally fleeting pains like illness, adversity, or poverty. Rather, it lay in the stillness of a well-developed and upright character.

The concept of *virtue* as a rational guiding principle is decidedly at odds with the modern secular sentiment, but the value of Stoicism is still discerned by readers who seek a deeper, more lasting source of wisdom. The goal of the Stoic was not mere "happiness" in the superficial sense, but a life well-lived. To live such a life requires:

- **self-control**: discipline and the refusal to be ruled by fleeting emotion,
- **wisdom**: a mature blend of logic, reason and rationality,
- **virtue**: fully developed moral standards of character, such as temperance, justice, and patience.

One classic Stoic maxim is that we should all strive to **"Have the *serenity* to accept what cannot be changed, the *courage* to change what we can, and the *wisdom* to know the difference."** When a man's perceptions, actions, and will are well-disciplined, then he can see the world as it truly is. He can relate to others in fruitful and productive ways, and he can use his own will and power to live in accordance with *good*, allowing him to prosper.

If our quest is to understand the mindset and attitudes of the quintessential high achiever, then we can begin with no better model than Aurelius. While this book asks, "What makes someone successful?" Aurelius took the question further and asked, "What *is* success? What *is* an excellent human being?" The answers he arrives at are not mere abstract philosophy, but intended to be put to use in practical, everyday principles of living.

Marcus Aurelius the man

Marcus Aurelius (full name, Caesar Marcus Aurelius Antoninus Augustus) was born in April 121 AD in prestigious Caelian Hill, to a wealthy and noble Roman family. Like most in his class, he was classically educated by reputable home tutors and taught to read and write in both Greek and Latin. His grandfather served as consul and prefect of Rome, his aunt was married to a future emperor, and his grandmother was due to inherit enormous wealth from her family.

Aurelius was certainly destined from birth for leadership and privilege, but his path to becoming emperor was actually more a matter of luck. At the age of 17, despite controversy, he was adopted by Emperor Pius Antonius at the request of Emperor Hadrian. Following Hadrian's death later that year, and the death of Pius Antonius 23 years later, Aurelius assumed the throne under the name Antoninus Pius, ruling jointly with his brother.

In the meantime, Aurelius studied philosophy. His teacher, Fronto, was a prominent scholar at the time and Aurelius would maintain a deep friendship with him for the rest of his life. Aurelius was especially inspired by the works of Epictetus and Seneca.

In 145 AD, during his second term as consul, the 24-year-old Aurelius married his cousin Faustina the Younger. The couple would go on to have 13 or 14 children, although many of these children lived very short lives. As emperor, Aurelius managed a complex and fractious empire. He dealt with Egypt's rebellion, deadly plagues, and wars against various Germanic tribes. In the winter of 175 AD, Faustina died. Five years later so did Aurelius, although so suddenly that many suspected poisoning. His son Commodus succeeded him.

Biographical details have been largely unreliable, and not much is known about Aurelius' private life. However, it is clear that he showed an early love for Stoic philosophy, and if we understand *Meditations* as a collection of private journal entries and notes to himself, then we can see that his was a diligent, passionate soul, eager for a deeper grasp of life's highest and truest principles.

The modern world often feels bereft of true leadership, morally adrift, and overburdened with confusion, chaos, and countless calls to distraction and self-indulgence. In many ways, however, the Roman empire Aurelius inherited was no less bewildering and complex. Marcus Aurelius' genius stemmed from his deep understanding of exactly how to maintain calm, controlled serenity in the face of it all.

Granted, we are not Roman emperors or consuls, but with Stoic philosophy, we too can cultivate the same practical emotional resilience, virtue and moral courage–regardless of the condition of the world around us.

Aurelius' commitment to Stoic principles and radical self-control powered his leadership

Aurelius understood that power without discipline would corrupt. His devotion to Stoicism taught him that the only true control *was over one's own mind and reactions*. When faced with betrayals or crises, he would turn inward to his "inner citadel," examining his judgments and stripping away emotional reactions. This Stoic practice of emotional mastery allowed him to lead with reason rather than passion, making decisions based on virtue rather than vengeance or fear.

The dominant worldview of ancient Rome was built around an objective moral dimension that could be accessed by man's observation and rational thinking. What would threaten this correct perception, however, was man's "passion," i.e., undisciplined emotions, impulses, or vices.

The world today tells us a story where human "happiness" is merely the indulgence of the senses, comfort, or instant gratification. Modern self-help and personal development culture sometimes emphasizes a "follow your bliss" principle, and tells us that the fulfilled human being is one who has every impulse validated, every desire satisfied, and every emotion revered and elevated to the status of truth itself.

For Aurelius, the exact opposite was true. Contrasting with modern life, the Stoic ideal was built on discipline and restraint. So, are we to be emotionless robots? No; Aurelius advises us to be "free from passions, but full of love." It is not that strong emotions, automatic

and emotionally because of what we think *should* be the case, but isn't. The other side of the coin is being in full possession of a will and a capacity to act upon our environment in order to change it for the better, and yet failing to act because, again, we are prevented not by reality itself but by our own distorted perception of that reality.

During his reign, Marcus faced constant crises, from plagues to invasions to betrayals, not to mention multiple deaths in his own family. Yet through Stoic practice, he was able to *maintain perfect clarity about what was and wasn't in his control.* By focusing solely on what he could influence–his judgments, his actions, his responses–he avoided wasting energy on futile resistance to reality. This energy could be more fruitfully applied to all those things in life where he *could* reasonably make a difference.

Both emotional resistance and apathy are matters of inelegance; when we act only on those things we truly can change, *and* we gracefully accept those things we cannot, we can rest in the peace of knowing that we have done all we can. We have lived well.

This is the key to resilience, self-governance, and poise. Wisely discerning the realistic limits of your sphere of control will help you manage whatever life throws at you with magnanimity, courage, and presence of mind. Aurelius writes, "if you are distressed by anything external, the pain is not due to the thing itself, but to your estimate of it; and this you have the power to revoke at any moment."

In his world, man's first concern is to adopt the highest and most rational attitude, and then to take moral action to live life according to that perception, given external limits and opportunities. Peace, the Stoics believed, comes from correctly engaging with the nature of reality itself, and that was primarily an activity of the mind.

If a man can see clearly, think reasonably, and act accordingly, then he has mastered himself. What is realistically and truthfully within your sphere of control? Act on those things, and withdraw your energy and attention from those things that will not change no matter how much you fret and resist them.

Transform your mind into your inner citadel

Marcus's Stoicism taught that true power lies in mastering your own mind. Start by creating a morning ritual of Stoic reflection: Before checking your phone or doing something else, take 10 minutes to write down what might trouble you today, Remind yourself that only your judgments about these events, not the events themselves, can disturb you.

In life you will encounter obstacles and setbacks, difficult people, and dangers and adversities of all kinds. What really matters, however, is not the absence or existence of these things, but your reaction to them. Look squarely at the thing that is bothering you and ask, "Can I really control this?"

Whatever your answer, there is something valuable to be gained. If you *can* control it, then apply yourself to thinking of meaningful actions you can take, and be thankful for the opportunity to cultivate courage. If you *cannot* control it, then be grateful that you have the opportunity to develop the virtues of patience and acceptance.

Take control of your experience and deliberately choose to focus on the beauty of life, on the options you do have, and on gratitude. High achievers may be "hungry" people driven by a desire to improve things, to grow, and to change–but they cannot go far unless they also possess a willingness to gently accept certain facts that will never be budged, no matter how ambitious or strong they are.

Your Inner Citadel is a private, mental kingdom in your own mind where you rule as sovereign. Constantly remind yourself of the power you do possess: the power to put your attention where you see fit, the power to resist vice and temptation, the power to alter your thoughts, and the power to act.

- When friends gossip, practice the Stoic pause; ask yourself "Is my opinion about this necessary?" Like Marcus examining his thoughts each night, build an impregnable fortress of mental discipline. Sometimes, discipline simply means the commitment to be fully *present* in every interaction, rather than reacting out of sheer momentum, habit, or peer pressure. Just pause. Come into the moment.
- Every time you feel a strong emotion, deliberately ask yourself about the situation at hand, and be honest about what is and isn't in your sphere of control. This isn't as straightforward as you would imagine—we often have extremely unrealistic expectations of both the world and ourselves. If, for example, a thunderstorm cuts short an

event you planned, pause and ask what you can do about it. You didn't cause the rain, nor can you cause it to stop; guilt or anger about it will only waste time and energy. Instead, have the discipline to keep drawing your attention to what you can control: your Plan B.

- When encountering someone else's strong emotion, take a moment to discern for yourself what is *theirs* and what is *yours*. If someone doesn't like you, for example, let it go, and do not allow their estimation of you to become yours. Likewise, just because an email says 'URGENT!' doesn't mean you have to panic; likewise, the existence of a temptation doesn't mean that you have no choice but to indulge in it.

Practice the art of acquiescence

Marcus wrote that what happens to us is fixed and inevitable, only our response is variable. When your plans get derailed, practice Stoic acceptance: State clearly "This has happened, what can I do about it?" Got rejected from your dream school? Say "This is now reality; what paths are still open to me?" Like Marcus facing plague or war or death, don't waste energy fighting unchangeable facts. Channel it into action within your control.

- Be grateful. "Do not indulge in dreams of having what you have not, but reckon up the chief of the blessings you do possess, and then thankfully remember how you would crave for them if they were not yours." If you're feeling sorry for yourself, have the discipline to instead tally up all the blessings you may be overlooking–blessings that could have just as easily been denied you.

- "There is never any need to get worked up or to trouble your soul about things you can't control. These things are not asking to be judged by you. Leave them alone." If you repeatedly find yourself upset or overwhelmed by things that you read in the news or on social media, for example, remind yourself that your engagement with these things is 100% optional. You do not *need* to have an opinion on every matter. You do not *need* to form a response to every stimulus the world throws your way. Find peace in simply tuning out those things that actually have nothing to do with you.

- Realize that you can **always** take courageous, rational, and moral action, no matter the circumstances around you. "Do the right thing. The rest doesn't matter. Cold or warm. Tired or well-rested. Despised or honored. Dying... or busy with other assignments... Look inward. Don't let the true nature of anything elude you... when jarred, unavoidably, by circumstances, revert at once to yourself, and don't lose the rhythm more than you can help. You'll have a better grasp of the harmony if you keep going back to it." Don't be dismayed at what the world is or isn't; if, for example, you are insulted, find comfort in the fact that you need not descend to insults yourself.

See every obstacle as a test of virtue

For Stoics like Marcus, every setback is an opportunity to practice virtue. Life itself can be seen as an enormous arena, or a laboratory, in which we embark on the continual project of developing and refining our characters. It's all "grist for the mill" in the sense that it doesn't matter whether the experiences that fate throws your way are "good" or "bad," life–*all* of it–can be a teacher. What matters is our willingness to learn, adapt, and grow in wisdom in the face of these inevitabilities.

- When someone cuts you off in traffic, treat it as a pop quiz in patience. When a friend betrays you, see it as a master study in forgiveness. Like Marcus using battlefield hardships to practice courage and self-discipline, turn daily irritations into your personal Stoic training ground.
- When you frame your efforts in terms of virtue, instead of "success" or "failure," you free yourself to find the upside in every circumstance. You can always be courageous, consistent, and disciplined, whether you pass an exam or not, for example. With a

Questions for reflection:

When I consider the things that distress and bother me in my life right now, how much can I realistically control?

What virtue can I cultivate in myself today–in this moment–regardless of how current circumstances are making me feel?

Today, might there be something that I need to evict out of my "inner citadel"?

Archimedes

"Give me a place to stand and a lever long enough, and I will move the world."

- **Archimedes**

Few of us know about Archimedes of Syracuse and the details of his life, but almost all of us know precisely what is meant by the expression "Eureka!" It is fitting that we now turn our attention to the life and mind that gave rise to the world's first "eureka moment", as it were.

A eureka moment is a flash of insight, a sudden moment of understanding, or the sensation of being struck all at once with the solution to a long-standing problem. The "aha!" moment is a flash of genius, where comprehension instantly clicks into place, and it's as though we are touched by the muses, or struck by a lightning bolt from the gods themselves. In our epiphany, we suddenly see things so clearly we wonder why we never saw them before. The resulting joy and satisfaction can literally make us exclaim out loud. "Aha! I've got it!"

So, who is the man behind this everyday phrase, and what can his story teach us about our own achievements? Archimedes of Syracuse (c. 287 BC–212 BC) was an ancient Greek mathematician, inventor, and physicist whose genius laid the groundwork for modern engineering and science. Celebrated for his contributions to geometry, mechanics, and hydrostatics, Archimedes also developed war machines that defended Syracuse from Roman invaders for years. His famous principle of buoyancy and methods for approximating pi exemplify his ability to blend theory with practical application. Even in his final moments, Archimedes' unwavering focus on his work symbolized his lifelong dedication to knowledge and discovery.

Archimedes was certainly a high achiever, but we have understand *how* he scaled those intellectual heights. To understand the story behind Archimedes' special flash of insight is to understand much of what characterized his life.

The story starts in Syracuse, an ancient Greek city which once appointed Hiero as a young general to command them during a war with Carthage. In a great battle in 265 BC, Hiero led

Syracuse to victory, so they elected him King. To thank the gods for his fortune and commemorate their triumph, Hiero commissioned a golden crown to be placed in the temple. He weighed out an amount of gold and hired a goldsmith to fashion the crown in the shape of laurel wreath–a symbol for victory.

The goldsmith went away and returned with a crown he presented to the king. It fit the specifications and weighed the same as the gold originally given. Pleased, Hiero paid the goldsmith, who went away. However, rumors began to circulate that the crown, though it weighed the same, was not in fact pure gold. It was suspected that the goldsmith had cheated the king by replacing some of the gold with cheaper silver, and pocketing the difference.

Hiero could not give an impure offering to the gods, and so had to find out the truth quickly. He summoned his own cousin, a young man of just 22 years old. This was Archimedes, who already had a substantial reputation for genius in mathematics and natural sciences. The king instructed him to determine if any deception had occurred, i.e., determine the composition of the crown–and do it fast.

Archimedes stewed and pondered for a long while. In those days, science was still at its rudimentary basics, and there really would have been no method to quickly determine the exact composition of any metal alloy. But what Archimedes *did* possess, however, was his brain. Taking a quick break from the riddle, he walked to the public baths one day, still turning the problem over in his mind again and again.

He stepped into a full tub of water and noticed that as he did so, an amount of water splashed over the rim. When he lowered more of his body into the water, still more was displaced. In that very moment, the answer to the problem of the golden crown struck him, and he leapt out of the bath again, purportedly running out into the streets naked yelling "Eureka!" (which means, "I have found it!" in Greek).

What had he found, exactly? Well, all at once Archimedes had discovered a method for measuring the volume of irregularly shaped objects. If you immerse an object in water, the water displaced will match the volume of that body–just like he did in the bathtub. The volume of the water displaced would exactly match the volume of the immersed object, no matter its shape.

However, Archimedes also realized another key piece of the puzzle: Volume is not the same as density. So, a pebble has greater density than a cork even though they both may have the same size. Archimedes already understood that gold was denser than silver. This means that if you have a lump of gold of a certain weight, and a lump of silver of the same weight, then the gold will be smaller in volume than the silver.

If the goldsmith hired by the king had indeed been deceptive and stolen some of the gold he was given and replaced it with cheaper silver, then the combined volume of gold and silver in the crown would turn out to be greater than the volume of the original amount of gold (because the silver would necessarily have a greater volume). But although Archimedes knew the volume of gold the goldsmith had originally been given, how was he going to measure the volume of the crown? While it *could* be melted down, the king forbid any harm come to it.

Thus, Archimedes needed a way to measure the volume of the crown, a highly irregular shape... Eureka!

It's at this point in the story that we can assume Archimedes put some clothes on and sat down to work to confirm his hypothesis: He confirmed the weight of gold that had been given to the goldsmith. Then he took a lump of both gold and silver of the same weight each, and placed them in a container of water, so he could precisely measure how much water was displaced by each. Were the amounts different? They were. The gold displaced less water, meaning it had a smaller volume.

It was time to try the experiment with the crown. Remember, the crown weighed the same amount as the weight of the original gold. He lowered the crown into the container of water and measured the amount of water displaced. If the crown was indeed pure gold, like the lump of pure gold, then it should be the same volume and displace the exact same amount of water. However, when he measured the water, he discovered that the crown displaced *more* water.

The experiment was conclusive: This crown, because it had a volume greater than pure gold of the same weight, was likely mixed with a less dense metal, i.e., silver. The king had been cheated by the goldsmith, who was then immediately put to death. The end.

Now, this story was never actually found in Archimedes' book, *On Floating Bodies*, but was recounted in various forms in other texts written in the first century BC. In truth, the story is quite likely apocryphal and never happened, but there is some truth nevertheless in its essence. Very little is known about Archimedes the man, but what survives of his legacy are his works and inventions, which are substantial: mechanical designs for claws, screws, levers, and pulleys, not to mention mathematical proofs and theories still relevant today. It's the Eureka story, however, that captures something very special about the problem-solving process.

Archimedes' innovative problem-solving redefined practical applications of science

Known for translating mathematical principles into practical solutions, Archimedes transformed abstract concepts into working solutions. His inventions ranged from the Archimedes Screw for lifting water to devastating war engines that kept Rome's armies at bay. Archimedes' genius lay in his ability to *practically apply* all that he learned and discovered.

There is an elegance, for example, in the story of the golden crown; Without using complicated instruments or tools, Archimedes solved the riddle using only logic, observation, and a rudimentary experiment.

It's no wonder that this story captures people's imaginations to this day–it is a model for truly intelligent problem-solving, and shows us the raw power of thinking clearly and rationally about the puzzles we encounter in life. Mathematics, engineering, and common-sense problem solving in the real world all come together to form an approach that is almost beautiful in its simplicity.

Archimedes combined open-ended curiosity with obsessive hard work and focus

Archimedes was known for becoming so engrossed in his mathematical problems that he would forget to eat. This intense focus was what led to his groundbreaking discoveries in geometry, physics, and engineering. Even at the moment of his death, he was so absorbed in solving a mathematical problem that he reportedly told the Roman soldier who killed him, "Do not disturb my circles!"

Archimedes was not a free-floating daydreamer, nor was he a joyless workaholic. Rather, he possessed that unique quality that has seemingly belonged to all high achievers, geniuses, and "nutty professor" types all throughout history: the ability to become so fully absorbed with your work that you scarcely remember that other things exist, let alone get distracted by them!

Cultivate your own "eureka" moment

Today, we speak about eureka moments as though they were purely passive experiences of illumination, completely outside of our conscious control. Archimedes discovered the solution to his problem, we are told, when he was on a break and *not* trying to solve the problem, right?

While this is true in a sense, Archimedes then took that singular flash of insight and ran with it, immediately following it up with active, conscious, and deliberate efforts to expand on that understanding. What's more, he laid the groundwork for that flash of insight by stewing over the problem for days. While it is true that insight can find us in the most unexpected places, it almost always tends to alight on those minds that have already been primed with plenty of pre-thought and contemplation.

To take inspiration from Archimedes, we need to understand the vital interplay between two forces: the active, conscious effort of hard work, and the passive, unconscious processes that occur outside of our control. By alternating hard work with rest, focus with open-ended thinking, and effort with release, we can increase the chances that we stumble upon a eureka moment of our own.

- Use breaks and rest strategically. A break is not just "nothing," it is a chance for your mental and physical resources to replenish, and for your mind to digest and process everything it has taken in. It is often during these restful moments where your brain suddenly puts things together, spots the solution, or cracks the code. If you're struggling with a problem, literally imagine just handing it over to your unconscious mind and take a break. Go for a walk, do something else, or even take a nap. Come back with fresh eyes. One great tip is to review a challenging question before bed, then "sleep on it." You'll be surprised by how often you wake up with a totally new perspective on things!

- Cut down on noise and distraction. Modern man's eureka moment is the "shower thought" because the shower is one of the few places where his attention is not captured by screens and devices. Give your brain a chance for productive rest. Give it an opportunity to generate its own ideas, rather than constantly bombarding it with external stimuli to process. Do "nothing" sometimes. Showers and long baths are good, but you can also just sit outside and watch the trees, or doodle. Don't always be rushing to the next task, and try not to automatically fill "empty" time with a distraction. Eureka moments need *quiet*.

- Honor your random insights and epiphanies by writing them down when they happen. Keep a small notebook at hand for quickly jotting down ideas as they occur to you, and take your random questions and wonderings seriously. You can set up a back-and-forth dialogue between your conscious and unconscious mind: take note of what your relaxed, unfocused mind comes up with, and then work on those things deliberately and consciously. Then, hand everything back to the unconscious again. Let those updated ideas rest and consolidate once more, before repeating the cycle.

Get lost in what you love

Archimedes was so absorbed in his work that he'd often lose track of time entirely. While he had gone to the public baths for a break on that fateful day, he had done so with a head full of ponderings and questions. However, Archimedes was not someone who forced himself to do a bare minimum of work hours, or tried desperately to convince himself to be more disciplined and productive. In fact, it would have been harder for him to *stop* working on a problem once he had sunk his teeth into it.

Many of us have problems with procrastination. We struggle to maintain consistent motivation or struggle with a lack of inspiration. We avoid starting our work, and when we finally do get started, we are instantly distracted, watching the clock, looking forward to when we can stop again.

The hard truth is that nobody can achieve much in this life if they have a reluctant or even resentful attitude to the goal they're attempting to achieve. The things we are consistently drawn to with passion and focus are the things we end up amplifying and developing over time–this is bad news for those of us who consistently allow our attention and focus to be hijacked by worthless endeavors.

Most things worth doing are difficult, and take effort and discipline. It is essential to be honest with yourself if your chosen goals inspire absolutely no energy or passion at all. While extreme and obsessive dedication to a task is probably not necessary, it's worth identifying those activities in which you truly can get lost for hours, and yet scarcely feel that a minute has passed. These activities are most likely those closest aligned to your truer purpose and talents–not to mention they're the things that you're most likely to get done!

- Find a task so engrossing that it makes the rest of the world disappear. Think back to the last activity you did without being asked or paid, and where you barely felt the hours whizzing by. What were you doing? How were you doing it? If you figure out exactly what it was that caught your attention, you can figure out ways to replicate that dynamic.

- It may sound obvious, but if you're "on a roll," don't forcefully stop yourself. You may have scheduled an hour guitar practice, for example, but find that you are enjoying yourself so much at the one-hour mark that you don't want to stop–so don't!

- Even our passions can be a drag sometimes, but it's often just a question of getting started and staying with a task long enough for our own natural momentum to kick in. If you're wrestling with procrastination, promise yourself to do *just one minute*. Inevitably, you'll find that that minute goes by really fast, and once you've begun, it's pretty easy to keep going.

Turn theory into action

Archimedes didn't just think about water displacement for fun, he used it to solve the king's crown mystery. Apply your knowledge to real problems. Just as there is a distinction between theoretical mathematics and real-world applied mathematics, there will be a distinction in your chosen field of study.

Solutions and theories that are meaningfully connected to real-world problems will always be more robust. Challenge yourself to stick to time limits and other constraints, and even if you have to impose artificial limits on yourself, keep asking how your work fits into the world, and its practical application.

- Whatever you're trying to learn, find ways to anchor it in your everyday life. If you're trying to learn more about social media algorithms, actively find ways to help your friend's small business grow, for example. If you're figuring out more about organization, don't be purely theoretical, but get your hands dirty and transform your roommates' chaotic kitchen or office into an efficient space. Like Archimedes, make your ideas *physically*

46

real. You'll learn more and you'll learn more quickly.

- As soon as you possibly can, test out your theories. Don't stay too long in hypotheticals or guesswork, but do experiments and appraise things for yourself. If you're considering launching a new business, for example, don't spend months planning and daydreaming–get out there and immediately start chatting with people, offering a lean/minimal version of your product or service, and gathering usable feedback.

- Change statements into questions. For example, instead of saying, "There's no way to measure the volume of an irregular shaped object," say "*Is* there a way? Why isn't there a way yet? If there was a way, what would it look like?" Questions like this are useful because they *prompt action*. You could idly wonder about something for years, but you'll only make real progress when you ask an outright question and take action to answer that question for yourself.

Michelle's story

Michelle was quitting her job in six months. She had known for the longest time that she wanted to set up her own business, work for herself, and earn her own income on her own terms. She had already acquired all the relevant new qualifications and training, she had brushed up on her basic business literacy, created a rock-solid business plan, and secured ample startup costs.

But there was one thing that still terrified her: marketing. Michelle was smart and hardworking, but she hated self-promotion, and she was unfamiliar with and uncomfortable using social media. Though she had great faith in her business idea, she was dreading "putting herself out there" and finding clever ways to win customers and clients.

She signed up for a much-recommended marketing course and paid all the right professionals to teach her how to reach her target market and start making sales. She learned more than she cared to about email marketing, SEO, building a website, creating content, cultivating a brand image, figuring out pricing, building an online presence…

The trouble was, whenever Michelle sat down to try and make sense of all this, it was like pulling teeth. She'd focus for a few moments but then get distracted by a phone notification or a friend dropping by. Being in her 50s,

Michelle was feeling increasingly daunted and overwhelmed at the technological challenges she faced.

Her social media accounts stalled and stagnated, and her marketing campaigns went nowhere. Bombarded with younger, more tech-savvy competitors crowding out the social media space, she became increasingly aware of her digital disadvantage, and grew discouraged. How was she ever going to find customers? Would she have to pay thousands to a marketing firm?

Her friends and family gave her plenty of advice and support–after all, they'd championed her business idea from the very beginning and believed in her, fervently–but as her last day of work loomed closer, her anxiety grew. She found herself increasingly unable to even go online, and just thinking about marketing filled her with dread. She began to procrastinate; she'd guiltily shirk all the boring social media stuff and go out in the evenings instead–book club, bridge, the movies, coffee with friends–it didn't matter, as long as she could avoid the marketing!

But then came her eureka moment. Michelle was at a church function one evening with two dozen other women from the community. Michelle was an active and engaged friend; she volunteered, hosted events and fundraisers, and spent almost every day doing something, whether that was a bake sale for the school, a casual get-together, or a group hike.

There she was in a crowd of women, explaining at length how she was having difficulty attracting clients. "How am I going to let people know about my business?" she was saying. "I hate social media and I'm so bad at it. I have no online presence at all, and no social network..."

And then it hit her. She was literally telling all this... *to her extensive social network*!

While she had wasted time and effort trying to learn how to market her business online, she had completely missed the fact that she had a sizeable social network right under her nose. She was *already* good at marketing.

For decades. Michelle has been a skillful communicator, and was a master at making real-world connections in her neighborhood. She'd often lose herself in the buzz of a busy event, chatting to people, making introductions, negotiating, planning, doing committee work... Michelle knew positively hundreds of people. Not only had she been "marketing" to them non-stop for months, but it had worked; several people were already interested in her service and were eager to refer people they knew to Michelle.

Thousands of years ago, Archimedes invented the **principle of the lever**. A lever is any bar that rests on a pivot or fulcrum that multiplies force applied on one end to the other end. With a lever, a man can shift a boulder many times heavier than his unlevered effort could manage. In other words, a lever is a simple machine and a "mechanical advantage device" that allows you to produce more force than you put in.

Michelle's eureka moment allowed her to identify the crucial levers in her own life, i.e. those places where a little effort would shift a big load. She multiplied force when she learned how to "leverage" her own pre-existing social network. Many problems in life are *not* solved by simply increasing force and effort, but rather by identifying crucial pivots and levers, and applying yourself in the world in direct, practical ways.

Michelle did not need to run naked through the streets to have her epiphany, but it was no less profound than the proverbial Archimedes. For Michelle, a single realization had changed her entire approach, and that realization came from a completely unexpected place!

Archimedes' high achiever mindset: "Stillness is the foundation of insight. At rest, I do my greatest work."

High achiever traits: Creative and productive rest, total absorption in work, applied insight, theory married to action.

- The passive, unconscious, and restful mind is a source of creativity and problem solving; cultivate eureka moments by making room for it to generate sudden insights.
- Fully immerse yourself (pun intended) in your challenges and projects. Pour energy into those things that make you lose track of time.
- Never be purely theoretical; genius happens when theory is applied, solutions are implemented, and insight inspires action.

Questions for reflection:

Am I leaving enough space (mental, emotional, physical) for a spontaneous eureka moment to find me?

Is there an insight I have already received, but have failed to take inspired action on?

Stop and think for a moment. To solve a problem I am currently grappling with, how can I leverage what I *already* have?

Michaelangelo

"If people knew how hard I worked to get my mastery, it wouldn't seem so wonderful at all."

- **Michelangelo**

Michelangelo (full name Michelangelo di Lodovico Buonarroti Simoni) was born in 1475 in Caprese, Italy. A renowned polymath who completely reshaped the artistic and architectural landscape of Western civilization, Michaelangelo continues to hold his position as one of the towering figures of the Renaissance. Famous for masterpieces like the statue of David, the frescoes of the Sistine Chapel, and the majestic dome of St. Peter's Basilica, Michelangelo combined prodigious talent with an obsessive drive for perfection. Yet his genius wasn't born from effortless brilliance alone; it was forged through tireless labor, radical experimentation, and an unrelenting pursuit of artistic truth.

To say that Michaelangelo was a high achiever is almost an understatement. He was not just a painter, sculptor, architect, and poet–he was an *exceptional* painter, sculptor, architect, and poet. When people speak of a "Renaissance man", they are often envisioning Michelangelo, or at least a master cast in Michaelangelo's image.

The young Michelangelo, the second of five sons, moved to Florence as an infant. His mother, Francesca Neri, sadly died when he was just 6 years old. She had been ill for a time, and Michelangelo had been placed in the temporary care of a family of stone masons. Remarking on this time of his life, he commented, "With my wet-nurse's milk, I sucked in the hammer and chisels I use for my statues."

A few years after his mother's death, he began his formal schooling and eventually became apprentice to the painter Domenico Ghirlandaio. Here, he was introduced to the world of painting, in particular, the technique of *fresco*, where the paint is applied directly to wet (or "fresh") lime plaster. At only 13 years of age, the young boy's talent was already obvious, although he was far from a showy child prodigy. After just a year, and on the recommendation of Ghirlandaio, the young painter came to the attention of Lorenzo de'

Medici, the ruler of the Florentine republic. Under Lorenzo's patronage, the young Michelangelo furthered his work and study, earning a reputation for himself as a virtuoso of singular talent and sensitivity.

Under the Medici name, Michelangelo's career really flourished, and he was soon making inroads into the glittering Florentine social elite. He met famous scholars, poets, thinkers, and artists, and through his connections was given the opportunity to study under the master sculptor Bertoldo di Giovanni. The Catholic Church gave him special permission to make anatomical studies of cadavers, and indeed this privileged influence is said to have manifested in his characteristic style: structural, muscular, detailed. Ironically, under Michelangelo's eye and hand, these anonymous cadavers were resurrected into sketches and paintings that continue to impress us with their startling life and warmth.

However, this prosperous golden era did not last, and when Lorenzo de' Medici died in 1492, the complicated political turmoil that followed forced Michelangelo to flee to Bologna. He was just 17 years old but had already lived a grand and impressive life. He continued to work and study, eventually returning to Florence in 1495.

Though much has been written about Michelangelo the artist, comparatively less is known about Michelangelo the man. He was known to be an eternally dissatisfied perfectionist and a depressive, with a fiery temper to boot. Though he had the luck to be cherished and promoted by one of the most powerful men in Italy early in his career, he also had his fair share of critics. In fact, rival Renaissance man Leonardo da Vinci (who is also on our list) claimed that Michelangelo's male nudes were so overly muscular that they resembled "bags of walnuts," and he plainly condemned the *David* statue's genitalia.

He had a permanent facial disfigurement from a blow he had received from a fellow school student he had taunted, and as an adult he endured serious physical strain bringing his artworks to life, especially the Sistine Chapel, which required endless hours of contortion, paint in the eyes, cramps, and exhaustion. In one of his writings, he explains, "I am here in great distress and with great physical strain, and have no friends of any kind, nor do I want them; and I do not have enough time to eat as much as I need; my joy and my sorrow/my repose are these discomforts."

As he grew older his lyrical impulse expressed itself increasingly in poetry and writing. His literary works are less well known but no less poignant, and they paint the same picture of a serious, solitary soul. No matter his wealth or fame, Michelangelo was known to live in squalor and showed little concern for his dress or material comfort. He would sleep in his worn-out work clothes, and often forgot to bathe. He was a devout Catholic all his life, claiming, "The true work of art is but a shadow of the divine perfection. Only God creates. The rest of us copy." Michelangelo believed that his sculptures already existed within the marble, created by God. His role was to remove the excess marble and reveal the divine creation. Gazing at his works, it's easy to imagine that this is precisely what happened.

Although Michelangelo never married nor had children, he was dedicated to Vittoria Colonna, herself a devout and noble widow. She was the muse and recipient of many of Michelangelo's 300 poems. Their enduring friendship provided significant comfort to Michelangelo until Colonna's passing in 1547.

Unlike many artists of his caliber, Michelangelo enjoyed fame and fortune during his lifetime, and lived to see his works embraced and revered by the world. In 1564, not long before his 89th birthday, Michelangelo died after a brief illness in Rome, and was laid to rest at the Basilica di Santa Croce. His legacy lives on in marble and stone.

Obsession: an engine for technical mastery

Michelangelo was talented, but that did not mean that his accomplishments came easily to him. In fact, though it's fair to say that Michelangelo may well have been blessed with heaps of natural talent, it's also true that he worked more than any of his contemporaries. The Sistine Chapel is stunning and a mere gaze is all it takes to appreciate its beauty; yet Michelangelo *spent roughly 18 hours a day every day for over four years in order to paint it.*

Consider for a moment the kind of discipline and effort this must have required. Michelangelo actually fired all his assistants at one point and decided to paint the entire 65-foot ceiling alone. He went up the extensive scaffolding and painted it all by hand, neck craned, paint dripping in his eyes. He would often just sleep where he was, on that very scaffold, and wake to continue where he had left off.

It is easy to say that certain people achieved great things simply because they were born with talent, but how many of us are willing to work *that* hard for *that* long? Michelangelo was not just talented. He was obsessed with his work, and this allowed a depth and intensity of focus that fueled all his achievements. He was the last person to rest on his laurels and assume that innate talent would be enough–really, it was just a start.

In order to paint well, he required a depth understanding of human anatomy. Images in a book weren't good enough; he would need to dissect actual human corpses so that he could paint with real perception and accuracy. He was unwilling to delegate even small tasks to others, and so got involved in everything himself: the quality of his paint, the nature of the light falling on that paint, the exact manufacture of his tools... he is said to have spent two years hunting down *precisely* the right shade of blue pigment for certain works. This manic dedication to understanding his materials and subjects at the deepest level enabled him to inject unprecedented life into mere stone and paint.

But his attitude can show us something important about the nature of achievement and excellence. Though obsession comes with obvious costs, it is a powerful source of energy and intention that can be directed towards the things that matter most. Many people desire success and achievement, but are completely unwilling to sacrifice the smallest comfort to gain it. They have completely unrealistic expectations around the path they will need to walk. They have "priorities" (when really, if it is a priority, by definition there can only be one!) and they attempt grand projects and ideas, but only with the leftovers of their time and energy. They imagine that raw aptitude is not only necessary for achievement, but also sufficient. Thus, we call Michelangelo a *genius*, and not a *tirelessly diligent and hard worker.* But he was more the latter than the former.

Michelangelo had monk-like focus, and ruthlessly eliminated distractions

How long would it have taken Michelangelo to paint the Sistine Chapel had he committed to just an hour or two a few times a week? How long if he painted only when he felt like it or "had the time"?

Under Michelangelo's obsessive 18-hour workdays, it took three or four years (let's say, roughly 21 000 hours). But if he decided that he also needed to go to gym, to read, to watch TV, to cook and clean, to work, to game, to socialize, to have a lazy Sunday morning once a week, to commute, to take care of the kids, to paint the living room, to walk the dog, to go to the dentist etc. etc. then he might have managed, say, 3 hours a week. Now, four years may seem strenuous, but under this regimen, it would take around *145 years*. In other words, it would take longer than a natural human lifespan. Think about that for a moment.

These figures are merely illustrative, of course, but the point is clear: **There is no achievement without intense focus.** You may waste years of life–or your entire life–on lukewarm effort that ultimately goes nowhere. Granted, you might not be willing to forego taking care of your kids or going to the dentist, but the good news is that your life goals are likely to be less ambitious than Michelangelo's!

Plainly speaking, the modern mind expects a smoother, easier path than the one we repeatedly see being taken by all the great achievers of antiquity. Real achievement is, by its nature, going to require action beyond the ordinary. Bruce Lee believes that "The successful warrior is the average man, with laser-like focus." Even if you don't possess much natural aptitude, it doesn't matter; channel and direct whatever you have towards a *single purpose* and it will become stronger and more forceful.

This means being honest and strategic. Focus is about being deliberate and intentional about where you choose to put your resources. Will this come with a cost, and will it entail some sacrifice? Of course. But you get to choose the sacrifice you make; what is important enough that you are willing to sacrifice for it?

Sleep in your work clothes

Michelangelo slept fully dressed on a wooden plank near his scaffold, rising instantly to capture ideas. This wasn't just about saving time; it was about maintaining unbroken creative momentum. Rather than dilute his time and energy with endless to-and-fro, he chose *one* task, and committed himself to that task alone.

"Sleeping in your work clothes" is about cutting out those time-wasting transitions that comes with "task-switching." Every time you shift attention or change focus, it comes with a cost, whether that's physically moving somewhere or changing clothes, or whether it's the mental and emotional gear change that costs precious time. Distracted multitasking splits up your energies, scatters your attention, and weakens your impact.

You don't have to literally sleep in your clothes, of course, but be mindful of ways you might remove any useless distractions, clutter, and inelegancies that prevent you from settling down into deep work.

- Set up a microphone next to your bed to capture song ideas the moment you wake. Keep your coding setup running 24/7, with problems deliberately unsolved before sleep so that your brain keeps working.

Like Michelangelo's paint-stained clothes, make the boundary between life and craft permeable. Install a whiteboard in your shower. Put a notebook in every room. The goal isn't workaholism–it's removing the artificial barriers between inspiration and execution.

- Don't task switch. If you can, schedule one task per day, or at least commit the day to the same *type* of activity, so you aren't pulled in multiple directions. For example, do all your writing or content creation on the same day, or dedicate a solid four or five hours just to musical drills or focused athletic practice. Flitting between tasks will keep your efforts shallow and ineffective; aim for prolonged, intense sessions instead.

- Be ready. Try to cut down on "set up" costs, whatever your goals are. If you're a painter, ensure that your materials are ready to go with minimal fuss; if you're studying an academic course, make sure all your books and papers are in easy reach; if you're mastering cooking or car repair or leather work, have a well-organized space that you can quickly slot into and get to work. Don't give yourself any opportunity to dawdle or procrastinate!

Your workshop is a sanctuary–protect it

Despite patronage from popes and princes, Michelangelo lived in stark simplicity, choosing to channel all energy into his work. His studio was legendarily austere–just bare walls, essential tools, and raw materials. This wasn't about aesthetic minimalism; it was psychological warfare against distraction. Design your creative space with the same militant focus. No inspirational quotes, no comfort objects, no shrines to past achievements. Just you, your tools, and the unfinished work staring back at you.

- Keep only what serves the craft: If you're a writer, one screen with no internet browser. If you're a musician, instruments and recording gear, nothing else. The space should make you slightly uncomfortable, like a warrior's tent before battle. You don't want it to be comfortable–your comfort zone is your enemy, after all.
- If you have doting patrons, be thankful for them, but if you don't, be ruthless in guarding your boundaries and keeping out anything and anyone who threatens the depth or intensity of your work. Clearly tell friends, family, and colleagues when you are and are not available, close the door, set up automatic email replies, turn notifications off, go somewhere quiet, or

put up a Do Not Disturb sign. However you do it, be clear first within yourself that distraction and disruption are the enemy, and you do *not* intend to let them gain ground.

- You don't want your workspace to be too cozy, i.e., a place where it's too easy *not* to work. At the same time, arrange things so that the easiest thing to do in this place is work–indeed, it should be the only thing you can do. If you're meant to be practicing the trombone, for example, do it in a room where there's literally nothing else to do but play the trombone. No snacks, no clocks to watch, no phones, nothing. You won't have to use willpower to fight off tempting alternatives if there simply aren't any.

Dissect your cadavers

Consider for a moment what it would be like to dissect a human body. Most med students find the experience somewhat harrowing and, though they do get used to it, feel powerful visceral reactions at having to literally peel apart a dead body. Michelangelo was only a teenager when he first began to do anatomical studies of dead bodies, but in addition to the instinctive recoil we all feel towards corpses, Michelangelo had to contend with something else: it was illegal.

He conducted his dissections in secret in the Monastery of Santo Spirito in Florence under special permissions and concessions, and, as a devout Catholic, would have also had to contend with the strong moral taboo around desecrating the sanctity of a human body in this way. In other words, there was a lot to push against: the law, religious taboo, and likely his own squeamishness. And yet, he did it.

We can learn a lot about "dissecting" all those things in our own line of study that make us flinch a little (breaking the law excepted!). To draw an analogy, high achievers tend to have a high threshold for looking closely at themselves, and the things they're trying to achieve. They're not scared of them. They don't flinch at the scary stuff.

Squeamishness around our own failures and blind spots can actually make us less effective over time, even if in the short term it feels more comfortable. Michelangelo took a painstakingly detailed and almost clinical approach to understanding *everything* about his work. While it must have been rather gruesome to look at bloody tissues, organs, and bones, Michelangelo was able to take insights gained from his observations to create beautiful depictions of those same bodies, only ones that appeared glowing with life.

- Don't be afraid to dissect your own performance and output. If you're terrified of public speaking, for example, film yourself daily in increasingly difficult scenarios: an empty room, one friend, small group, hostile audience, etc. Review each video with brutal detachment, several times. Map your voice patterns. Graph your filler words. Track eye contact duration. Turn performance anxiety into a fascinating research project where you're both scientist and subject. It'll be cringeworthy at first, but you'll get used to it!
- If you're struggling with a concept or topic, don't get frustrated. Slow right down, and go into the details. If you're trying to understand a complicated physics or math idea, for example, stop and make sure you properly understand all the supporting concepts and definitions first. Imagine carefully explaining the concept to a five-year-old, diagram it out, or go back to foundational resources to make sure you're fully understanding the deeper "anatomy" of the problem.
- If you've received some negative feedback, correction, or criticism, stay calm. Try not to let emotion overwhelm you, and avoid the temptation to fall into anger, defensiveness, or denial. Closely

considering negative feedback is painful, and you really won't *want* to do it... but if you can, you will be rewarded with exceptional insight and the chance to improve. Does your critic have a point? What do they see that you don't?

Emily's story

Emily was one of those people who had been saying "I want to write a novel" for seemingly her entire adult life. One day, she was struck with the realization: Unless she actually *did* something about this long-held dream, a dream is all it would ever be. She would leave this earth never having written that book. So she set herself some goals. She got fired up and decided that this time, she'd do it for real.

Like most of us, however, Emily's life was full to the brim of everyday mundanities that seemed to constantly get in the way. She would sit down to write in the evenings, and the cat would scratch at the door to be let out. She'd hear her kids fighting in the other room. As she wrote, her eyes would be constantly drawn to the dozen open tabs on her internet browser, or her incriminating To Do list. Then a package would arrive, so she'd have to stop writing and get up to answer the door. Then the washing machine would ping, so she'd take ten minutes to quickly fold the laundry. Then she'd made herself a cup of tea and sit down again. Then her phone would beep. *"Can I call? Kinda urgent"* the message would say...

In this same way, Emily's daily hour of writing quickly evaporated, and after a month she had little to show for it. She despaired.

Was it not possible to be a normal person with a normal life and write a novel? For a while, she grew resentful and took solace in that old writer's excuse: "I don't have the time." One evening, however, Emily was watching TV (always time for that, right?) and came across a documentary about Michelangelo painting the Sistine Chapel. Again, it hit her like a ton of bricks: How could she write her novel if she wasn't prepared to, well, *write it*?

The next morning, she took action. She maxed out all her annual leave and booked her own "writer's retreat"–i.e., a tiny cabin in the woods with no hope of internet access. She would go alone and she would work as hard as she could, for as long as she could, and write like her life depended on it. Her family protested and her friends expressed doubt, but what did she care? This was important.

After three hard weeks, Emily returned a different woman. Her eyes were strained, her hands were cramped, and she was utterly exhausted. She had spent day after day in that cabin, in her pajamas, living off toast and coffee, her every waking moment dedicated to the book and nothing but the book. But she had written it.

It still had a few rough edges, yes, but it was *done*.

Michelangelo's high achiever mindset: "I am a block of marble, and with patient diligence, I will chip away at the irrelevant, to reveal my purpose."

High achiever traits: Intense focus, dedication, fearlessness, deep work, and precision.

- Forget about talent, aptitude, or "genius"– just work as hard as you can on a *single* goal.
- Proactively cultivate an internal and external environment free of distractions and diversions.
- Instead of recoiling from failure, criticism, or difficulty, get curious about the details, set your feelings aside, and learn what you can.

Questions for reflection:

When everything is said and done, what is truly the single thing I care most about?

What can I do today to draw clearer boundaries around my work sanctuary?

When was the last time I was fired up with obsession for something? What can I do to dissect–and maybe replicate–that experience?

Hippocrates

"There are in fact two things, science and opinion; the former begets knowledge, the latter ignorance."

- **Hippocrates**

Hippocrates (c. 460-375 BC) often revered as the "Father of Medicine," was a trailblazing figure who transformed healing from a practice steeped in superstition into a disciplined and ethical science. In an era when illness was often attributed to divine punishment or malevolent spirits, Hippocrates charted a new course by observing symptoms, identifying patterns, and seeking natural explanations for disease. This empirical approach laid the groundwork for clinical medicine as we know it today.

Yet Hippocrates' legacy extends far beyond his clinical methods. He established medicine as a noble profession rooted in moral responsibility, manifested by the now ubiquitous Hippocratic Oath—a guiding ethical framework still referenced in modern medical practice. His teachings emphasized the sanctity of patient welfare and the duty of care, raising the standards of medicine to a higher moral plane. In other words, much like Marcus Aurelius, Hippocrates' excellence was in the domain of *ethics*, and his contribution was to institute exacting professional standards in medicine.

Hippocrates was not just a practicing physician, but a philosopher; for example, he not only introduced the concept of prognosis (from the Latin *pro* meaning "before" and *gnosis* meaning "knowledge", i.e. making a pronouncement about the most probably outcome given current signs and symptoms), but taught its practice to his many students.

To really understand Hippocrates' contribution, we need to know a little about the context in which he lived. Though difficult to appreciate now, the very concept of formalized medicine as we understand it today is relatively modern. We have figures like Hippocrates to thank for introducing not just their technical expertise, but the ideological and philosophical framework of medicine as a science in itself. Having produced so many notable thinkers and natural philosophers, many of us might be surprised to learn just how spiritual ancient Greece was, and how closely human health was bound up with magic, divine ritual, ceremonial invocation, and more.

Without exaggeration, Hippocrates lived in a world where most people received medical care through physician-seers, witch doctors, shamans, priests, and mystics. Pre-Hippocrates, disease was often understood to have been caused by the indwelling of evil spirits, ill-fated astrological events, or the punishment of the gods. What was required for health was the re-establishment of cosmological order by, say, receiving an exorcism or making a burnt offering to the appropriate gods or spirits. The ancient Greeks knew practically nothing of physiology and anatomy (there is a long-standing taboo against human dissection, as we've already seen) and very little idea of what disease actually was, or how it developed.

Thus, Hippocrates' contributions were not just to improve the field of medicine; it was to *create* it. Because of Hippocrates' paradigm-shifting influence, today disease is understood to be of natural origin, and medicine therefore not a question of philosophy or religion, but one of natural environmental influences on the human organism. It's hard to emphasize just how radical a shift this was at the time.

In his (purported) book, *On the Sacred Disease*, for example, Hippocrates explains what really causes epilepsy:

"I am about to discuss the disease called 'sacred.' It is not, in my opinion, any more divine or more sacred than other diseases, but has a natural cause, and its supposed divine origin is due to men's inexperience and to their wonder at its peculiar character."

Though Hippocrates' attitude was ideal, his conclusions were nevertheless often false. For example, he did support humorism, which is the belief that the body is constituted from four compositional "humors"–blood (hot and moist), phlegm (cold and moist), black bile (cold and dry), and yellow bile (hot and dry). Humorism posits that disease will occur if these four elements are out of balance; therefore, to restore wellbeing, the physician needs to increase or decrease one or more of the humors accordingly, to re-establish a healthful equilibrium.

Thus, for example, a person with too much humoral blood (a "sanguine" personality) might require bloodletting. If too much black bile was suspected (a "melancholic" personality), on the other hand, the physician might suggest certain diet and lifestyle remedies to introduce more warmth and moisture to the constitution. Hippocrates' humoral theory was not unique in thinking of human beings in this way, and many traditional and alternative medical models today (such as Indian Ayurveda) follow similar principles.

Humoral theory was the "grand unified theory of medicine" for 2000 years, and was considered officially discredited in 1858. It was superseded by the "doctrine of specific etiology" (i.e., there is a specific and knowable cause of disease). Though Hippocrates himself was a proponent of humoral theory as well as many other now debunked ideas, he nevertheless brought to his developing field a *spirit of empirical enquiry and high ethical standards* that remain as his legacy today. Hippocrates' methods were still a far cry from what we'd recognize as modern medicine, but we would not have modern medicine today were it not for the groundwork he laid.

We do not know much about Hippocrates the man; the practitioners of Hippocratic medicine at the time were often conflated with the theories they advocated. A few details are tentatively confirmed: he learned medicine from his father Heraclides and his grandfather, also physicians. We know that he travelled widely and his name spread with his teachings. Over time, Hippocrates became almost emblematic of the enlightened, quintessential modern physician, and his image and name came to represent the highest possible standards of systematic clinical study.

Hippocrates was radically empirical

Hippocrates is said to have commented, "All the most acute, most powerful, and most deadly diseases, and those which are most difficult to be understood by the inexperienced, fall upon the brain."

Though he meant it literally, we can also infer a figurative meaning: One of the most dangerous human maladies is to have a malfunctioning *mind*. Why? If we think poorly, are imprecise with words, confused, or self-deluded, everything we do next will invariably be distorted.

In philosophical terms, empiricism is a way to go about gaining knowledge and accessing truth. Empiricism is the belief that knowledge can be acquired via the experiences of the senses. Empiricism is a pillar of the scientific method and informs the logic of experiment. For example, if I observe (with the sense of sight and hearing) that a person's cheek breaks out in a rash every time they eat strawberries, I can make a guess (a hypothesis) that if they stop eating strawberries, they will stop getting the rash.

Here, my sensory observation (as well as a little rationalism thrown in) has allowed me to take my experience of the world and learn something true about it. The person has not offended the gods, nor is their facial rash a sign of being born under a "bad star." Using *only* our sense perception, we can plainly see what the cause is.

If this idea seems so obvious as to seem boring, consider that even today the threat of superstitious thinking lingers on, and more than 2000 years after Hippocrates, we are all still very tempted to reach for explanations that are simply not grounded in empirical fact. Consider, for example, that many alternative healing approaches today consider rashes a sign of psychological turmoil or spiritual distress. The skin, we are told, is an emotional and psychic boundary between self and universe, thus its lack of wellbeing is a message and a manifestation of certain negative energies, imbalances, and core beliefs…

Not a million miles away from humors, demons, and divine magic, right?

The point is that it is very, very easy to abandon experiential observation, logically proven and tested claims, and the factual reality that we see before our eyes in favor of ideas and explanations that *feel* right, but are completely unfounded. Pseudoscience, magical thinking, self-delusion, and superstition are not just things that ancient people succumbed to–we are all prone to such mental distortions.

Hippocrates built his professional legacy on the firm foundation of natural science and empirical observation. We can incorporate a degree of empiricism into our everyday personal lives, too, when we commit to bravely seeking and accepting the truth as we find it actually revealed to us, rather than as it appears to our imaginations, fears and hopes.

While others were blaming gods and spirits, Hippocrates carefully documented patient cases and searched for natural causes. He maintained detailed clinical records, studied anatomy through observation, and developed systematic approaches to diagnosis. This empirical foundation turned medicine from mysticism into a rigorous discipline.

Hippocrates established medicine as a sacred calling with ethical boundaries

Through his famous oath and teachings, Hippocrates defined medicine as more than a mere trade; it was to be a moral commitment requiring absolute dedication to patient welfare. He guarded medical knowledge zealously while paradoxically making it more accessible through his school, creating a tradition of excellence through mentorship.

He took his duty to his patients seriously. He made the time to observe and record their symptoms, to think carefully about the cause and expression of their disease, to logically arrive at a diagnosis, to treat diligently, and to use only tested and proven methods. Today, medical ethics is vastly expanded from Hippocrates' time, but the spirit contained in his original set of ethical guidelines remains.

To this day, the Hippocratic Oath serves as a noble standard of care. Traditionally, a newly qualified physician swears, in the presence of several pagan gods, to uphold a certain standard of treatment. He or she promises to respect patient confidentiality, to "do no harm" (non-maleficence), to respect one's teachers, to refrain from euthanasia and abortion, to protect trade secrets, and to refuse sexual relations with patients, to name a few specifics.

While the ancient text is traditional and highly symbolic, the oath is actually codified in the legal statutes of many jurisdictions, potentially resulting in criminal liabilities if broken. It may seem quaint to swear an oath to ancient gods like Appollo or Asclepius, but this aspect of the oath communicates an important part of its power: **the willingness to subject oneself to a higher authority**. In other words, this is greater than a law or a mere personal promise; it is a vow and a pledge to conduct oneself according to the highest possible universal principles. The work of a doctor, then, is beyond mere civic duty and concerns the realm of divine command–*that's* a high standard!

Make your practice a temple of truth

Hippocrates transformed medicine by rejecting irrational belief and inquiring instead into the natural causes of disease, as revealed to reason and to the senses. Hippocrates' worldview still had plenty of space for gods and demons (the Hippocratic oath, after all, is made to the likes of Hygeia and Panacea), however, he made inroads in establishing truth and empirical reasoning as the higher "gods" that he would serve.

No matter the area of your work, the skills you are attempting to master, or the kind of knowledge you yearn to acquire, you can imagine that you too have a "practice" and that it can be run on principles of radical empiricism.

- If you're trying to create or innovate, question every assumption. Much falsehood, confusion, and self-delusion slips in when we fail to examine our knee-jerk beliefs and expectations. Get into the habit of asking yourself: What do I know? How do I know that? For example, before automatically assuming that you're not making sales because your price is too high, consider other possible explanations. Might the price be too *low*? Don't guess, try to find out.
- If you're facing something unknown, avoid approaching it with mystical thinking and instead cleave to hard evidence and plain fact. If there is no documented evidence, then do your own experiments to find out! Test things, and don't be afraid of trial and error. For example, if you're launching a new business, conduct A/B testing, ask potential clients for input and requests, conduct interviews, and test out different possibilities first.
- Strengthen your own etiological thinking. When solving problems, look for root causes without getting distracted by overly emotional explanations and assessments. Every problem has a cause; understand what it is, and you are halfway to finding its cure, that is, the solution. If your job applications are constantly rejected, for

example, try not to take it personally, but try to understand what is actually happening, and why.

Document every step like sacred script

Hippocrates revolutionized medicine by meticulously recording observations and creating detailed case histories that became the cornerstone of medical learning. In your own field, adopt this principle by tracking every process, outcome, and insight—whether successes or failures. Identify patterns, refine strategies, and create systems others can learn from.

- Whether you're running a business, developing a creative project, or mastering a skill, treat your documentation as a living guide. Like Hippocrates' case histories that educated generations, your records should not only help you improve, but also serve as a roadmap for others to follow.
- Write your own code. Many professions have industry standards and legal codes, but you can always choose to go above the bare minimum, and set yourself *aspirational* guidelines, too. Don't just imagine these things, put them in writing. Set down your own written code of conduct, and put your promises into words.

- Be scrupulous when it comes to documenting the details. Record dates, observations, findings, goals, actions taken, results, and your interpretation of those results. The more thorough you can be, the less room there is for conjecture, guesswork, and memory lapse.

Create ethical boundaries before success tests them

The Hippocratic Oath wasn't just a list of rules and industry standards, but a system for maintaining integrity under pressure. For Hippocrates, physicians were bound by a duty to beneficence (helping patients), non-maleficence (not harming patients), justice, and respect for patient autonomy and dignity.

A doctor was not a mere technician of the body, but someone who would uphold the sanctity of human life, and serve with integrity, humility, honesty, compassion, and gratitude. What do *you* stand for, and how do you manifest those things in your own work?

Too often, we neglect to think carefully about our own moral standards and only do so reactively when it's too late, i.e., when we're pushed into a corner or a boundary we never knew we had is violated. Instead, proactively clarify for yourself what you stand for before you meet with forces that might push you off of that course.

- Literally sit down to spell out your ethical boundaries, whether it's personal or professional, general or specific. Start with a simple bullet point list: What won't you compromise on, ever? Where are your hard limits? What principles guide your work? What is important to you, whether others agree or not? If you struggle to do this, approach the question from the other angle; Who or what do you consider to bet a moral or ethical failure? Work backwards to discover what this tells you about your own values and principles.

- In life, there will always be the option to "cheat"–i.e., the easy way out, the convenient excuse, the not-entirely-honest tactic. Our greatest ethical commitment is to refuse to indulge in self-delusion. Sometimes, the right thing is not the easy or fun or pleasant thing, but we hold ourselves to it. High achievers not only have exacting ethical boundaries, but they're willing to apply those boundaries to *themselves*.

- Don't work alone. It's tempting to imagine that you alone are responsible for how you conduct yourself, but be like Hippocrates and establish for yourself a guild, a group who will hold you accountable and also offer support and inspiration. Look for professional bodies but also more informal meetups and social groups that will help you strengthen and clarify your resolve.

Jean's story

When Jean was little, she was told dozens of times, "Girls are bad at math." Jean was intelligent and worked hard in school, yet so completely did she internalize this belief that by the time she was in her early teens, she just "knew" that math was something she could never do. Eventually, she convinced herself she didn't even *want* to understand math.

Many years later, Jean found herself attempting to complete her first psychology degree, which required a daunting module on statistics and research methods. To her terror, she realized that whether she liked it or not, she would have to do math. All semester she wrestled with the material and, anxious beyond belief, the time came for the final exam—which she failed spectacularly.

Instantly, Jean spiraled into self-pity and despair. Why was life so unfair? Why should a psychology student be forced to complete this awful module? Jean felt that the entire system was against her, punishing her for what was after all not her fault. Over the following months, as the next statistics exam loomed closer, Jean grew more and more desperate and anxious.

Was all this drama a "sign from the universe" that she was on the wrong path? Maybe her "math anxiety" was a valid condition that nobody was taking seriously? Maybe God himself had it out for her, and her suffering was some kind of karmic payback... did she need therapy for her childhood trauma? Hypnosis? Should she just quit the whole degree?

She relented and hired an expensive math tutor. Within the first five minutes of the first lesson, the tutor asked casually to see a copy of the failed exam. Jean admitted that she had thrown it out. The tutor then asked her detailed questions about precisely what she was struggling with, where she had lost marks in the exam, and what she felt were her biggest blind spots. Jean could give no answer other than, "I don't know... I'm just bad at math?"

The tutor immediately brushed this off. "You're not bad at math. You just don't understand it yet. You've failed an exam, that's all. When we find out *why* you failed, we'll get to work putting it right."

Jean was taken aback. She had never thought of things this way before. But it was true; her entire mental framework was simply not based on empirical fact. "I'm not good at math" was a feeling, a habit, a guess. She didn't really know how good at math she was because, if she was honest, she had never really tried all that hard.

Over the next few months, Jean worked meticulously with the tutor; she took several mock exams and then analyzed them in detail, identifying exactly where her knowledge gaps were, then systematically working to build up her understanding, step by step. When she complained, "I can't do this!" the tutor asked her, "Is that a fact or an opinion?" When she got something wrong, her tutor would ignore her embarrassment and shame and simply ask, "Where exactly did we go wrong? Let's backtrack and see."

Jean realized that she had wasted time indulging in psychological and even supernatural explanations for her lack of success with math, when simpler, more objective explanations would do. The truth is, she was no better or worse at math than anyone else, and when she came out of the fear and darkness of her own personal superstition, she was free to just observe the facts of what was in front of her, and take action.

As she made concrete and practical gains in her learning, she also developed a more disciplined and clear approach to life's challenges. She realized that she could *enjoy* sitting with a math problem and puzzling it out, one step at a time. Even if she got a problem wrong, it didn't matter; no matter what, she could always turn up on time, work hard, and do her best, and this itself gave her an enormous sense of pride and achievement. Jean ultimately did pass her statistics module, but the work ethic she developed with her math tutor that year stayed with her for the rest of her life.

Hippocrates' high achiever mindset: "I pledge a solemn vow to pursue the true and the good in all things."

High achiever traits: Rigorous empirical thinking, high ethical standards, professionalism, honesty.

- Set your sites on truth and intellectual rigor, and let go of the rest.
- In whatever work you do, be a scientist; document your every step and let diligent record-keeping reflect diligent thinking.
- Pair intellectual rigor with moral rigor–promise the highest principle your greatest effort.

Questions for reflection:

What higher authority or principle do I serve? And what vow might I make to that greater standard?

Might it be time to let go of some of my own personal superstitions?

Are there places where I need to clarify or defend my own ethical boundaries?

Leonardo da Vinci

"To develop a complete mind: Study the science of art and the art of science. Learn how to see. Realize that everything connects to everything else."

- Leonardo da Vinci

Leonardo da Vinci (1452-1519) transcended the boundaries between art and science, transforming both through his relentless pursuit of knowledge and beauty. While others mastered single domains, Da Vinci wove together anatomy, engineering, optics, and art into a unified vision of the world. His restless mind filled thousands of notebook pages with innovations centuries ahead of their time–from flying machines to human anatomy–while creating artworks like the Mona Lisa that redefined what painting could be.

Da Vinci is arguably the world's most recognizable polymath and Renaissance man, and his genius was for synthesis and connection. But who was he as a person?

Though there has been much open conjecture and speculation about his private life, da Vinci's story is clearly one characterized by insatiable curiosity. He was not just a painter, but an inventor, scientist, botanist, sculptor, draughtsman, philosopher, and musician... and somehow something that defied categorization altogether. The diversity, depth, and range of his talents suggest, like so many others in this book, a transcendent quality that goes beyond superficial categories and speaks to a deeper, more profound essence.

Leonardo da Vinci was born on April 24, 1452, in the town of Vinci, Florence. His father was Messer Piero Fruosino di Antonio da Vinci, a legal notary, and his mother was Caterina di Meo Lippi, a servant girl. Named "Leonardo di ser Piero da Vinci," his name means "Leonardo, son of Messer Piero from Vinci," with "ser" denoting his father's gentleman status. Since his parents were unmarried at his birth, Leonardo's family position was somewhat complex. He lived with his mother until age five, then moved to live with his father, who had married a sixteen-year-old. Leonardo's father had twelve more children through four different marriages, leading to fractious disputes over his estate after his death.

Leonardo's illegitimate status meant that while he was acknowledged as da Vinci's son, he received a very limited formal education. He was taught basic reading, writing, and arithmetic, but he learned from an early age to rely on his own powerful sense of observation. At fourteen, his father's contacts secured him an apprenticeship with master painter Andrea del Verrocchio, a student of the sculptor Donatello.

Leonardo worked diligently and eventually became a paid employee, embedding himself in the emerging Renaissance art scene with figures such as Botticelli, Ghirlandaio, Michelangelo (a later rival, as we've seen), Masaccio, and Perugino. Da Vinci assisted his master in painting "The Baptism of Christ," and legend has it that Verrocchio was so impressed when he laid eyes on the beauty of the angel Leonardo had created, that he quit painting himself and never took it up again.

At the time, the powerful Medici family controlled much of the city. In 1481, Lorenzo de' Medici commissioned da Vinci to paint an altarpiece for the Church of San Donato, a work never completed. Subsequently, da Vinci was employed by Ludovico Sforza, producing famous works including "Virgin of the Rocks" and "The Last Supper." He also painted for notable individuals, including King Louis XII of France. When Leonardo passed away at age 67, he made the astonishing claim that, "I have offended God and mankind because my work did not reach the quality it should have."

Da Vinci wielded systematic observation as his superpower

Da Vinci is reported to have said, "There are three classes of people: Those who see, those who see when they are shown, those who do not see."

The quote above exhorts us to "learn to see." Da Vinci didn't just look; he developed a complete system of seeing. He dissected over 30 human corpses in secret, studying muscles and bones until he understood the mechanics of every facial expression. He watched birds for thousands of hours, recording not just their flight patterns but their weight distribution and wing adjustments in turbulence.

Each observation connected to every other: The way water spiraled in a stream informed how he painted curling hair; the mechanics of human tendons inspired his engineering designs. His notebooks reveal a mind that transformed raw observation into universal principles, seeing the shared patterns that connected everything to everything else.

The world is now filled with Da Vinci's countless works that prove without a doubt that he was one who *could see.*

Da Vinci "alchemized the impossible"

Unlike his contemporaries who separated art from science, Da Vinci forged revolutionary insights by combining domains that no one else combined. When studying optics, he didn't just theorize about light, but invented sfumato, a painting technique that captured how human peripheral vision actually works. His anatomical studies didn't just document the body, but transformed into machines those human mechanics. His famous "mirror writing" wasn't mere eccentricity, it was a systematic tool for seeing familiar things from radical new angles (and also, for keeping things secret!). By refusing to accept the boundaries between fields, he created works that seemed to bridge all categories, and transcend reality itself.

"Only connect"

EM Forster's novel Howard's End concludes with the following:

> "Only connect! That was the whole of her sermon. Only connect the prose and

the passion, and both will be exalted, and human love will be seen at its height. Live in fragments no longer."

Forster's main character came to the conclusion that a person's main motivation in life should be to connect the *passion* (i.e. the inner life, curiosity, purpose) with the *prose* (the outer life, the works). The result will be a fulfilment of both.

Though Forster's novel was primarily about the difficulty of creating connections across different social classes, the narrative is filled with the theme of connection of all kinds, and the phrase *only connect* has itself come, rather aptly, to represent the power of connecting diverse ideas, themes, and insights.

Da Vinci was certainly not a man to "live in fragments." Instead, he connected everything he learned with everything he already knew, building complex mental webs of knowledge. **These connections are ultimately all driven by curiosity, which is, in its own way, a kind of love–love for the unknown, and for the joy of learning.** According to Da Vinci, "verily, great love springs from great knowledge of the beloved object, and if you little know it, you will be able to love it only little or not at all."

- Link up everything with everything else, and let passion be your guide. Start a "Da

Vinci notebook" where you map unexpected connections. If you're reading about psychology, draw lines to that cooking show you just watched; how does understanding human behavior change how you'd present a meal? If you learn about marketing, connect it to the nature documentary you saw; how do animals attract attention? Make it practical: Create a simple grid with two columns. In one, list things you're learning or experiencing. In the other, force yourself to find three surprising ways each connects to your main goal or project. Like Da Vinci connecting water flows to hair curls, train yourself to see patterns everywhere. Let the love of curiosity drive you.

- Don't just make connections between the different ideas you encounter, but connect the *passion* to the *prose*. Constantly ask yourself how your growing knowledge connects to your identity as a person, your values and principles, your hopes and fears, your ethics, your purpose.

- Make friends with metaphor. **All true artists are medium-independent**, meaning they can express themselves through any medium, whether it's words, images, stories, data, color, food, movement, music, dialogue... *anything*. Indeed, artists like Da Vinci will happily connect one medium to another, or look for interesting relationships between the two. What connects your piano practice with your sessions in the gym, for example? What does your sales pitch look like as a classic Greek myth? If you had to *invent* a whole new medium for your unique message, what would that actually look like?

Turn curiosity into detective work

Da Vinci never had the option to quickly Google an answer to a question about human anatomy, nor could he watch a YouTube video to understand a painting technique or learn about artists living on the other side of the world. In Da Vinci's time, there were no commercial art stores where you could buy readymade paints, nor readily accessible science or biology books.

Instead, the world was filled with mystery and the unknown, and the only way to get a hold of it was to actively ask questions, seek, explore, pick things apart, test things, or, if what you needed didn't yet exist, *make it yourself.*

- Pick one everyday mystery that intrigues you: Why do some houseplants thrive while others die? Why do certain social media posts go viral? Create a simple investigation system: First, document the pattern you notice. Then, list three possible explanations. Finally, design tiny experiments to test each theory. If you're studying plant growth, track sunlight patterns, measure water amounts, photograph leaf changes. Make each question a mini research project with real data.

- The next time you have an idle question, write it down somewhere, perhaps in a dedicated "question book." Challenge yourself not just to quickly pull a superficial answer off the internet, but hunt out rich, meaningful answers that genuinely expand your understanding. Follow your curiosity–one question tends to lead to another! If you're at a loose end, rather than zoning out with TV or mindless scrolling, generate a random Wikipedia article and make your own question-guided treasure hunt (just type "Special:Random" into the search bar until you find something that captures your curiosity).

- If you're struggling with something or you've identified a knowledge gap, resist the urge to seek an immediate answer from others. Spend some time with the problem and challenge yourself to devise your own answers or solutions first. Da Vinci made all his paint and ink from raw materials himself–you could do the same. Rather than relying on "ready-made" materials, tools, software, systems, or even ideas, be resourceful and make your own.

Draw before you think

Da Vinci insisted on drawing everything before trying to understand it. He wouldn't just observe a flower, he'd draw every petal's curve, shadow, and vein. This wasn't about art, but about *seeing reality clearly*.

- Create your own practice of "drawing before thinking": Before writing a business plan, sketch your idea in simple shapes. Before solving a problem, map it visually. Use basic diagrams, stick figures, or flowcharts–artistic skill doesn't matter. The goal is to see what's really there, not what you assume is there.
- You can inject some of this Da Vinci spirit by simply playing around with different mediums. If you're trying to solve a visual problem, put the problem into words. If you're trying to solve a verbal problem, see what it looks like acted out or converted into metaphor or symbol. You get the idea. Sometimes simply "switching channels" on a problem allows us to see and understand its other dimensions.

- Change perspectives. A great exercise for art students is to turn an object upside down and sketch it that way. The idea is to look beyond all your preconceived ideas about how all the pieces come together, and just draw what you actually see. Any time you look at something in your world without preconceived ideas, you are doing the same, and you can often comprehend it better because you're approaching it without assumptions and expectations.

Anna's story

When Anna was called in to independently re-evaluate the brand strategy for an underperforming soy milk product, she could tell at once that the company was underestimating the size and nature of the problem. Having been in marketing for more than two decades, Anna had earned a reputation for excellence that was uncommon in her field.

During her first meeting with management, she tried to understand what the company was doing, why they were doing it, and the results they were getting. The company already had an inhouse marketing team, a group of talented creatives, and a whole stable of seasoned advertising pros... yet they had all failed to make a success of this one product:

the company's soy milk offering. It would be Anna's job to find out why, and fix the problem.

However, whereas the company were expecting a few design tweaks or a clever ad, Anna knew better, and she went away to chew over the problem in detail. It was a mystery she didn't yet know how to solve, but she would. Why were all this household brand's products selling well *except* their soy milk? When worldwide consumption of dairy alternatives was higher than ever, why was this company failing to appeal to customers?

Anna set out to investigate, and she approached her work like Da Vinci approached his. She sat down and brainstormed freely, drawing connections and looking for patterns. She realized with surprise that none of the people behind the brand design were vegans themselves, even though the product's target market was vegans. She studied the existing brand–the product itself, the packaging, the aesthetic–as though she were studying a fine art masterpiece that held the secrets to the universe.

There was something about this problem that nobody else was seeing, and Anna knew she'd have to devise her own solution outside of what the company was already doing. Not being a vegan herself, she approached the entire concept from scratch, as though she was an alien who had only just heard of the idea for the very first time. She looked at everything with fresh eyes. What did vegans actually *want*, anyway? The company clearly had an idea of the priorities and values of the average vegan, but were they actually correct? What did the world look like from a vegan's perspective? And what was going through that vegan's mind, start to finish, when they actively decided not to buy the company's soy milk?

She conducted painstaking interviews. She read market research data about the company's demographics, she pored over important papers, considered various case studies, and closely picked apart the company's vision statement. But she went far, far beyond this. Anna knew that to understand the performance of this single product, she would, in essence, need to understand nothing less than human nature itself.

What was the deeper psychology behind veganism? What were the foundational ideological underpinnings, and how did that actually look, translated into words and colors and images? She created mood boards, mulled over the logo design, visited vegan forums, read reviews, and learned a little about the politics of package design (yes, really!). She investigated the history of certain typesets and lettering conventions, dabbled in architectural principles to better understand the carton's spout design, and explored the psychological implications of including a cute little cartoon cow as brand mascot.

Like an anthropologist, she paid detailed attention to the language, imagery, and style used by vegans when they communicated with one another, and the manner in which they expressed their own preferences. Like a linguist, she explored not just visual communication, but the total social, economic, cultural, and psychological profile of this particular soy milk. Phew!

To keep track of all these inquiries, Anna took rich notes and made sketches. She paid attention to tiny details and quickly did a crash course in the psychology of fonts, did a little comparative study on the shades of green used by competitors, and even learned about the soy plant itself, and how it as cultivated. She considered the cultural reception of the symbol of the cow across the globe, and how certain messages were received depending on a nation's religious and political orientation. Throughout, she made connections.

When she met with company management, she was ready. She did not merely present an updated brand strategy for the soy milk; she presented an entirely new concept that fit with a sophisticated new vision of their ideal customer. She explained the core problem: The current brand emphasized how great soy milk was *as a dairy milk substitute*. All the branding emphasized how impressive it was that the milk was indisguisable from dairy milk, and was just as nutritious, just as delicious.

But Anna's investigations and connections had produced real insight: Their vegan customers simply did *not* think this way. They did not consider soy milk a replacement, but a food in its own right. In fact, by comparing soy milk to "normal" milk and emphasizing that it was "just as good," the company was unwittingly sending the message that there was something central about dairy milk, and implying that soy milk was an aberration that could only be accepted to the degree to which it successfully mimicked dairy milk. Anna reasoned that vegans, whose entire philosophy rested on the feasibility of a plant-only diet, would resent this implication. For certain vegans, milk requires no substitute, because milk is nutritionally and philosophically unnecessary.

Understanding this, Anna explained that everything about the product had to change.

The brand image needed to promote the benefits of soy in its own right, without reference to dairy at all–no cute cow, no patronizing "just as good" claims. The changes were made, and Anna was vindicated. Within 6 months, sales of the soy milk had not just increased, but were soon *overperforming* relative to the company's other offerings. Anna achieved this success not because she was good at marketing, but because she was a modern-day polymath. Her skill was to connect marketing to *everything else.*

Da Vinci's high achiever mindset: "Only connect."

High achiever traits: Creatively linking and connecting, curiosity, transcending mediums and formats, true "mixed media".

- Step outside the artificial boundaries dividing fields of study, and look for creative areas of overlap and connection *between* them. Life itself is not divided this way, neither should your investigation of it be.
- Play with format. Freely mix verbal, visual, cultural, scientific, artistic, etc.
- Aways be curious. Look at things with fresh eyes.

Questions for reflection:

Concerning a problem I'm currently facing, how would I solve it if I were looking at it with Da Vinci's eyes?

What am I most curious about today?

Can I convert some of my current questions, ideas, and thoughts into a completely different format?

Aristotle

"The educated differ from the uneducated as much as the living from the dead."

-   Aristotle

Born in 384 BC, Aristotle is easily one of the most influential philosophers and scientists of all time. He is widely considered the last in the long line of classical Greek philosophical tradition, which spanned hundreds of years. Bestowed with the grand title "the Father of Logic," Aristotle is today so closely associated with the art of philosophy itself that his image and name have come to resemble the very human endeavor of which he was such a notable example–rational thought.

Greek philosophy continued well after Aristotle, and he was followed by the Epicureans, the Skeptics, the Stoics (of which Marcus Aurelius was exemplary), and Plato's academy, but much of this flourishing philosophical thought owed its existence to the foundation of Aristotle's work. Aristotle–along with Socrates and Plato–dominated the fifth and fourth century Athenian intellectual arena, and their work set forth dialogues, theories, ideas, and conversations which had paradigm-shifting effects that are still rippling throughout the modern world today.

A student of Plato and teacher of Alexander the Great, Aristotle transformed the very way we think about and attain knowledge. **He combined empirical observation with logical analysis**. His systematic methods of inquiry remain integral to modern science and philosophy to this day. We tend to think of Aristotle as a philosopher, but he was truly a polymath and applied himself to the investigation of *all* of life–the natural sciences, linguistics, politics, the arts, literature, psychology, ethics, rhetoric, and economics, to name a few.

Aristotle was a "renaissance man" before the Renaissance, and his genius was not merely to apply his mind to this or that field, but rather to explore and expand the very concept of thought itself. Clear, rational, and logical thinking can be seen as the ultimate competence, since it is a skill that can be endlessly transferred to *any* human domain where we wish to acquire knowledge and understanding.

As with so many ancient figures, it would appear that the more emblematic and legendary Aristotle's legacy became, the more his personal life shrunk into obscurity, and most historians admit today that very little is known about Aristotle the man. What we do know is this: He was born in Northern Greece (just outside Thessaloniki) during the classical period. His father was Nicomachus, personal doctor to the King of Macedon, and his mother was Phaestis from Euboea.

Raised in a medical household, Aristotle showed an early interest in the biological sciences, and was not only reported to belong to the early medical guild, the *Asclepiadae*, but to be descended from the legendary Asclepius himself–the god of medicine and healing. Both his parents died when he was just a boy, and he was raised by his guardian, Proxenus of Atarneus. At 18 he moved to Athens and entered Plato's Academy, where he quickly earned himself the nickname, "the mind of the school." He lectured and studied there until he was thirty-seven.

When the great Plato died, Aristotle left the academy, and in 343 BC entered the employment of Philip II of Macedon to tutor none other than Alexander the Great when he was just 13 years old. When Aristotle was 49, he set up his own philosophical school at the

Lyceum. In Ancient Greece, the Lyceum was a special temple dedicated to the worship of god Apollo Lyceus ("Apollo the wolf-god") and had long been the site of philosophical dialogue and debate. In Aristotle's day, the temple had fallen somewhat into decline, but Aristotle and his disciples did much to revive it.

His academy was called The Peripatetic School, so called from the Greek *peripatētikós*, loosely meaning *of walking around*. This may be because of the notable colonnades and walkways of the Lyceum, or because of Aristotle's purported habit of walking while he lectured–or perhaps a little of both. Like Aristotle himself, who was not a native Athenian, many philosophers were "metics" (free citizens of another state) and could not own property. Thus, the Lyceum became a vibrant free and public place for the meeting of great minds.

Life in an ancient Greek academy bore only a dim relation to our modern ideas about schools and universities. There was no curriculum as such, no entrance requirements, and no fees. Though there was an impressive library, lectures were informal and egalitarian; the aim was not to provide dogma or indoctrinate, but to explore and discuss.

During the roughly twelve years he led the school, Aristotle wrote extensively, but most of his treatises were never intended for publication. Even though only an estimated third of everything he wrote survived, this alone was responsible for radically changing the course of medieval scholarship. Muslim scholars called him "the first teacher," and early Christian church writers like Aquinas simply called him "the philosopher." His teachings and his method of inquiry were so distinctive and lasting that they were only significantly replaced during the Enlightenment of the 17th and 18th centuries.

Aristotle married twice and had one son, Nicomachus (after his father) and one daughter, Pythias. He was only 62 years old when he died, but his legacy lasted much, much longer, and his spirit still lives on in mankind's collective philosophical soul.

Aristotle anchored his understanding in observation

While his contemporaries often relied on abstract theorizing alone, Aristotle emphasized careful observation of the natural world. He dissected animals, documented embryonic development, and developed early classification systems, creating the foundation for zoology and comparative anatomy. His insistence on evidence-based conclusions marked a departure from the speculative approaches of earlier thinkers.

"Nature is like a woman who enjoys disguising herself" explains Aristotle, "and whose different disguises, revealing now one part of her and now another, permit those who study her and assiduously to hope that one day they may know the whole of her person."

With the careful use of logic, reasoning, *and* empirical observation, one could peer into the very nature of things, understand the causes of phenomena, and access by the disciplined and skillful use of our mental faculties the true character of existence itself. Though Aristotle was certainly a deep thinker, he did not limit his inquiry to what happened in his skull. Rather, the full package of human sensory experience may also be called upon in the quest to understand and master:

> *"Lack of experience diminishes our power of taking a comprehensive view of the admitted facts. Hence those who dwell in intimate association with nature and its phenomena are more able to lay down principles such as to admit of a wide and coherent development; while those whom devotion to abstract discussions has rendered unobservant of*

facts are too ready to dogmatize on the basis of few observations."

Aristotle united intellectual and moral excellence

"Educating the mind without educating the heart is no education at all."

- *Aristotle*

The field of philosophy that focuses on a human being's character and moral development is called virtue ethics, and we can thank Aristotle for laying its earliest foundations. While modern analytical philosophy has largely concerned itself with metaphysics, epistemology, language, and other cognitive endeavors, the earliest Greek philosophers were just as interested in understanding what constitutes the good and virtuous life. Aristotle, too, believed that man's inquiries into nature should also include questions about his entire life, the way he lived it, his beliefs and attitudes, and the higher principles by which he conducted himself.

It's important to understand that for Aristotle, however, "intellectual virtue" and "moral virtue" were not really separable. Wisdom was not only possible to discover and worth seeking out, but it was intrinsically connected to the development of one's moral character and mental habits. Human excellence, then, was a *total* condition encompassing practical wisdom, ethical decision-making, virtuous habits, clear thinking, and civic duty.

Aristotle believed that ethical virtue comes from habit, and that intellectual virtue arises from teaching. Teaching, he explained, was a question of disciplined experience over time. Education, if it is to be successful and lead to meaningful achievement, must thus be cultivated through both intellect and virtue, simultaneously.

For the ancient Greeks, there were broadly five intellectual virtues: *techne* (craftsmanship), *phronesis* (practical wisdom or prudence), *episteme* (scientific knowledge), *nous* (intuition and understanding) and *sophia* (philosophical understanding). Man is thus not just a thinker, but a doer, a maker, an asker of questions, an experiencer, and a free moral agent.

Now, while all of this may seem *theoretically* interesting, let's take Aristotle's advice and make sure we are not dwelling too long in abstract discussions. How can we educate ourselves in the Aristotelian sense, so that we are schooled not just in one area or another, but as total human beings?

Spy on your own life like a philosopher-detective

Do you know anyone who is very academically intelligent and "head smart," yet their actual life is in a total shambles? Might that person be you? Unless we are courageous and honest enough, then we will also lack intellectual courage and honesty, meaning we will get distracted and confused by our own lazy thinking, self-deception, and irrational fear.

If we learn anything from Aristotle, it should be that **we are only intelligent to the degree that we can practically apply our insights and understandings**. Purely theoretical, abstract knowledge is next to useless unless *applied*. Instead of getting lost in lofty and intelligent-sounding theories that keep you detached and aloof from your own life, make your life the first topic of investigation. While philosophers tend to expound on "humanity" and "truth," you may actually discover more power and clarity in thinking more specifically and concretely: not "humanity," but "me, as this specific human, right now."

- Pick an area of your life to investigate, whether it's why your mornings feel rushed or why certain projects never get finished. Track the details obsessively: How long do you actually spend scrolling your phone? What triggers procrastination? Use this data to design experiments, like setting strict screen-time limits or batching tasks. The goal is to uncover objective patterns and implement solutions that actually work, so that your observations are turned into practical breakthroughs.

- Ask questions, and keep on asking them. Think like a philosopher and constantly define your terms. When you say, "I want to be more productive" exactly what do you *mean* by this word, productive? What does that look like in the world? Although you don't need to re-invent the wheel each time, it can be incredibly illuminating to go back to first principles: What *is* productivity anyway? What am I trying to produce here? Do I actually have any reason to think this way about productivity in the first place?

- The roots of education may be bitter, but the fruits are always sweet. We can become extremely effective self-teachers if we are willing to let go of our own suborn tendency to cling to what we *think* is true, but isn't. Intellectual honesty means saying "I don't know" when we don't, readily accepting correction, and cultivating a preference for the logically sound over the emotionally appealing.

Level up your intellectual virtues

Aristotle believed that **virtue and excellence were a question not of innate character, but of *habit*.** While puzzling over life's big philosophical questions can be fun, the only way to acquire real-world, practical excellence is to get your hands dirty, and to do it consistently. *Virtue is a process*, and it unfolds day by day, hour by hour.

- Choose a specific virtue, like bravery, and create "mini quests" to strengthen it. For bravery, you might start by asking questions in meetings, then work your way up to giving a presentation. For generosity, find one way each day to help someone, whether it's mentoring a colleague or surprising a friend with their favorite coffee. These intentional, repeatable actions transform abstract ideals into concrete strengths over time.

- Identify any emotional hang-ups that are getting in the way of you achieving your intellectual potential, then take proactive steps to mitigate them. For example, laziness, fear, and overwhelm are often at the root of poor work and study habits. If you want to improve your music practice, your efficacy at work, or your creative output, then, you need to pay equal attention to consistently removing laziness, fear, and overwhelm from your life. Make discipline, energy, and serenity equal goals, and pursue them relentlessly through good lifestyle habits, therapy, or stress management techniques.

- Above all, don't deceive yourself. "The worst of all deceptions is self-deception." The lives we live are not about what we think and imagine, but what we **do**, consistently, day after day. A high-minded ideal means nothing if it is never actually expressed in the way we live. One easy way to level up your own intellectual virtue, then, is to be relentless in rooting out any intellectual *vice*; drop from your life any habit rooted in blame, apathy, victimhood, denial, passivity, and the like. The next time you are arguing with yourself about why you don't need to go to the gym, for example, imagine Aristotle arguing back with you. Do you want to make excuses and idleness a habit? Or do you want to fight to make discipline your habit instead?

Test your ideas in real-world settings

Aristotle knew that untested theories are just wishful thinking. This applies both to our fanciful fantasies about life, but also our groundless worries and fears about it.

- Take an idea you're passionate about–whether it's a business pitch, a new diet, or a social initiative–and put it through its paces. Launch a prototype, gather feedback, and adapt. If you're studying leadership, volunteer to organize a local event and see how your ideas hold up under real-world pressure. The act of testing and refining your ideas ensures they become *actionable* wisdom.

- Get into the habit of not automatically taking your own word for it. Be relentlessly on the lookout for beliefs, expectations, and assumptions that really have no basis in fact or logic. Regularly consider your core beliefs and make them stand up for themselves in the court of reason. Is this really true? Do I have evidence for this? Take emotion out of it. For example, you may have talked yourself into a rather harebrained scheme for a new business, or you may have talked yourself *out* of a great opportunity. Whatever you're telling yourself, be clear about what is merely emotion, and what is supported by reason.

- The proof of the pudding is in the eating. You could waste years of your life ironing out a hypothetical idea in your mind, when you could have confirmed the validity of that idea in the real world in a single afternoon. It is easy to deceive yourself in your own mind, but harder to get reality itself to go along with a delusion. Be brave and take your ideas "to market" as soon as possible. For example, if you have a brilliant idea for a book or a service or a project, try out a smaller prototype first, before you sink time and energy into it, only to discover too late that the idea is basically unsound.

Michael's story

Michael had always been the classic high achiever–he had been the top performing student in every year since middle school, and nobody was in the least surprised when in 6th grade he announced a plan to go to med school. Michael's life seemed blessed and the road ahead looked full of opportunity. Except, it didn't quite happen that way.

Michael sailed through his undergrad college years with ease, but when pre-med was done and medical school proper began, things went awry. Michael had long known that his chosen route would be a difficult one–after all, this was a big part of why he had chosen it! But it was difficult in a wholly new, unexpected way.

While he had been prepared for ample sacrifice and hard work, he hadn't anticipated that his frustration would be with the process itself–poor communication, sky-high expectations, total lack of support, and the endless pressure to seemingly do the impossible. Michael had always been a star student, but he couldn't figure out the constantly changing rules of med school. It was a case of: "The rules are made up, they don't make any sense, we won't tell you what they are... but you will be heavily penalized for breaking them."

Michael quickly became discouraged and resentful of his tutors and lecturers who seemingly had little interest in what mattered. He was either overworked and stressed to death, or wasting time trying to figure out what was expected of him. He started to despair at the systems he was forced to work with, wondering how to reconcile his lofty goals to help people with the stupid and outright harmful patient protocols that he had no choice but to follow. Michael was soon bored of the red tape and senseless bureaucracy, and tired of being condescended to by superiors and ignored by noncompliant patients..

One day, Michael met a friend of a friend whom he discovered was also completing med school, but in a different state. She was relishing it, she said, and couldn't be happier. "Lucky you" Michael said. "You must have proper lecturers or something." But the other student laughed and said that her lecturers were impossible, the course work a headache, and the program a total disaster. Michael could not make sense of her attitude. The longer he spoke to her, however, the more he felt slightly ashamed. He couldn't put his finger on why, and mulled over their conversation for days afterwards.

It dawned on him slowly that in his training so far, he had felt a certain *groundlessness*. Unlike high school and undergrad, med school had no real blueprint. He was on his own. It was a shapeless, "make it up as you go" experience with no training wheels. Michael had become so demoralized by this that he had begun to blame everyone else around him for his failure to thrive. But he had to admit a hard truth: He was not taking responsibility for his own learning. He was used to following a path that was already laid out for him,. but now, the lessons were so much harder and more complicated, and he needed to fight to create his own order and purpose.

Instead of complaining about the quality of his learning materials, the lectures he was receiving, or the organization of the program he was being funneled through, why not take ownership of the process of developing his own intellect? Med school was a stressful mess, but then, wouldn't life be the same? If he hoped to be a doctor, then this was the real world that he'd need to learn to navigate.

So, inspired by the other student's attitude, he got tough with himself. He looked at his own life like a philosopher, and used the cold light of reason and rationality to pick apart his assumptions, his goals, his values, his options, and his limitations. He would no longer wait for the outside world to supply these for him.

Michael reconnected with his own deep ambitions, and challenged himself to live up to his own standards of intellectual excellence, regardless of what unfolded around him. He would not rely on a pre-made curriculum, but fashion his own, and he would do so in the real world. He set up independent study groups and volunteered, not waiting for direction or permission. When he felt that his training was incomplete or confusing, he asked his own questions, going beyond the given material if necessary.

If he couldn't understand something, he went back to basics and reasoned through it carefully. If he still struggled, he wouldn't despair that nobody was helping him, but rather asked more questions: Who can help me? What will my answer to this problem look like and where can I find it? If the learning opportunities provided by his college were lacking, well, he'd simply go out into the real world and seek a better learning opportunity there.

It was more work, yes, but it was also more *fulfilling* work, and he soon found himself less and less bothered by the ineptitude and ignorance of others, and more energized to become the professional he had always wanted to be. Michael was learning not just to be smart and effective, but to be wise, patient, and self-directed. His development in med school was qualitatively different from the training he'd received before. He had been a good scholar, but med school had challenged him to become something more: someone with intellectual virtue.

Aristotle's high achiever mindset: "I educate my heart as I educate my mind, and with rigor I achieve excellence in the school of life."

High achiever traits: Disciplined, rational and logical thought, intellectual virtue married to moral virtue, self-education, life experience.

- Take ownership of your own moral education, and conduct yourself with wisdom, prudence, patience, and disciplined curiosity.
- Commit to being your own teacher, and have the courage to hold your ideas up to

the light and see how they perform in the real world.

- Make a conscious habit of excellence, and don't wait for it to happen on its own, or be given to you by other people.

Questions for reflection:

If the ultimate goal is to be an excellent human being, where am I at currently in my "curriculum"? What do I need to do next to cultivate my own intellectual virtues?

Can I identify one thought, idea, assumption, or belief that has not earned its right to stay in my mind?

How can I put my abstract ideas to test in the laboratory of real life?

Marie Curie

"Life is not easy for any of us. But what of that? We must have perseverance and above all confidence in ourselves. We must believe that we are gifted for something and that this thing must be attained."

- Marie Curie

Marie Curie (born Marie Sklodowska ,1867-1934) revolutionized science through her groundbreaking discoveries. Her life was one of firsts and onlys–she was the first woman (indeed the first person) to win two Nobel prizes in two separate disciplines, and remains the only woman to have done so in human history. To this day, only five people have ever won two Nobel prizes, and just two people that have won them for two separate fields–Marie Curie and Linus Spalding. Truly, Marie Curie was a high achiever even amongst high achievers, and her contributions have yet to be matched.

Curie was a humble woman, yet she achieved unprecedented accomplishments: discovering two new elements (radium and polonium), pioneering the field of radioactivity (a term she coined), and becoming the first woman in France to earn a Ph.D. She wasn't just a theorist; she personally processed tons of pitchblende ore (a radioactive mineral that is the primary source of uranium) by hand in a drafty shed to isolate radioactive elements, demonstrating extraordinary dedication to hands-on scientific work.

During World War I, she revolutionized battlefield medicine by developing mobile X-ray units and personally driving them to the front lines, directly saving countless soldiers' lives. It is difficult to tally up the influence that Curie's work has had on the world, especially considering the way she both developed and championed life-saving cancer treatments.

Today, Curie's legacy inspires feminists the world over, who see in her a triumphant negation of stifling feminine domestication in a world that sees woman as intellectually inferior.

Curie was a radical; not just a radical woman, but a genuinely unique and remarkable human being with a spirit so animated by love for the unknown that she serves as an inspiration to this day–to men and women. Curie didn't struggle with gender norms; she *disregarded* them and applied herself to a more noble struggle, i.e., straining her intellect toward its very limits, and exploring the furthest outer realms of science.

So, dazzling scientific achievements aside, who was Marie as a person? She was born in 1867 in Warsaw, Russian occupied Poland. She was a child prodigy. Both her parents were teachers, and the value of education was imparted to her early on, with her father tutoring her in mathematics and science. It was clear that Marie should further her education, but real educational opportunities for women in Poland were non-existent at the time. She had initially set her sights on becoming a student at France's Sorbonne, but her family could never have afforded it.

In fact, the original plan was for Marie to work as a governess so she could earn money to send her sister, Bronya, to medical school. The idea was that when Bronya completed her education, Marie would have her turn. In the meantime she waited and earned a little money by working as a governess. Though she was already 24 years old when she finally made it to the Sorbonne to study physics and mathematics, she quickly took it in stride and excelled in her courses. In Paris, she was able to attend lectures by the great leading mathematicians and physicists and soak in the intellectual atmosphere.

Though she lived in a cramped, impoverished little apartment, she relished her freedom to throw herself completely into her studies. She wrote in a diary of this time, "It was like a new world opened to me, the world of science, which I was at last permitted to know in all liberty." At this point, her goals were simply to earn a teacher's diploma and return to Poland. Fate had other plans.

When she was 27, she met internationally renowned scientist and Professor in the School of Physics, Pierre Curie, and the two married a year later–supposedly, he had to propose three times before she agreed. The couple had a daughter, Irene, but they also collaborated extensively with one another, eventually being jointly awarded the 1903 Nobel prize for Physics together with Becquerel for their work on radioactivity.

That same year, Marie earned her doctoral degree, becoming the first woman to do so. The following year, she gave birth to her second daughter, Eve. Amazingly, this daughter was the only member in her immediate family to not pursue science nor win a Nobel prize. Her mother, father, and sister Irene would eventually all win Nobel prizes, as would her own husband!

Biographers have long held that both Pierre and Marie were idealistic, driven, energetic, and determined. The two were married, but their affinity for one another was as intellectual kindred spirits, and they built a humble life together based on their shared passion for their work. When Curie died of aplastic anemia on July 4, 1934, she was buried next to her husband in Sceaux, although their remains were moved in 1995 so they could be interred in the Pantheon in Paris.

The life of a real radical

Curie was known even during her lifetime for a completely singular attitude to her work; She was not afraid of the unknown or of new ideas. She introduced the theory that radiation originates from sub-molecules, which questioned the belief that atoms lacked sub-particles. This she appropriately called her "daring hypothesis." Not only was Curie an original thinker, but she was unafraid to freely communicate her insights and ideas, undeterred by controversy or other people's criticisms. Her work was frequently undermined, her abilities questioned, and her intelligence diminished. Many people automatically assumed that it was really her husband that was the brains of the outfit, so to speak.

She pressed quietly on, resolute. She was a diligent, hard-working woman who freely shared her ideas and reveled in collaborations with anyone who showed an interest in the work. She believed in herself and the work she was doing, and did not fear the unknown, but rather set to work trying to understand it. A humble and pragmatic woman; her goal was never personal aggrandizement or competition, but rather the pure scientific urge to touch the truth, and to understand something of reality. What's more, Curie took what she learned out into the world, so that she could make a difference to people's lives. She was not a mere academic, she wanted to discover and master tools that could truly benefit humanity.

Marie Curie turned personal hardship into shared innovation

Despite facing poverty, gender discrimination, and the tragic death of her husband Pierre, Curie refused to accept limitations. After Pierre died, colleagues assumed that Marie would quietly accept her widow's pension and abandon her work at the lab. But Marie continued on, and took the entire lab over herself.

She insisted on sharing her discoveries freely, refusing to patent them, and actively sought ways to apply her research practically. Her commitment to making science serve humanity showed how theoretical breakthroughs could be transformed into real-world impact. Today, we admire her all the more because of what she achieved while remaining grounded and humble.

Challenge conventional wisdom... with proof

Like Curie proposing radical ideas about atomic structure, don't be afraid to challenge established beliefs–but back your ideas with rigorous evidence. When facing skepticism, focus on gathering irrefutable proof rather than arguing. Let your results speak louder than words.

Push against boundaries and conventions, but do not waste time asking for permission from others, explaining yourself, or getting defensive when it comes to those boundaries and conventions. Don't rebel for no reason, but don't get distracted by other people's ideas of who you are and what you can and can't do. Just get on with doing the work that your convictions have inspired you to do.

- If you work in an industry or sector where you don't quite "fit," don't waste time *telling* people why you belong there.

Instead, *show* them with concrete achievements. Be the change. If as a "lady doctor" or "male nurse" you receive annoying comments or flat-out discrimination, have the last word by being genuinely good at what you do, without compromising who you are as a person.

- Take ego out of the equation. Curie was so effective because **she loved the truth and knowledge more than she loved being the special one to discover it**. She did not jealously guard her discoveries, nor was she possessive of her projects. She ignored mean-spirited attacks and cherished those who were willing to collaborate in good faith. Let the truth speak for itself. If, for example, you're stuck in an argument with a rival at work, refuse to go to war with them, and instead quietly set about finding out what is really the case. In fact, work *with* them to this end!

- Be ready to challenge conventional wisdom even within yourself. The next time you talk yourself out of taking a risk or trying something new, ask yourself whether you really "know" as much as you think you do about the matter at hand, or whether you're just making guesses and assumptions. Be a true scientist. For example, get into the habit of asking, "Do I

actually have evidence for believing XYZ?"
Then go from there.

Make radical bets on yourself

When others underestimated her, Curie bet on her own abilities, from working as a governess to fund her education to taking over the lab after Pierre's death. Conventional thinking is often fearful thinking–we are unwilling to take the risk of trying something that nobody else has done before, and, perhaps unconsciously, we opt for the easier, safer route.

Curie said, "Nothing in life is to be feared, it is only to be understood. Now is the time to understand more, so that we may fear less." When we hang back, second guess ourselves, or doubt our ability to face the unknown, we are actually demonstrating a lack of trust in both ourselves and the world. But when we bet on ourselves, we are refusing to let fear steer our lives, and instead give ourselves over to the spirit of learning and understanding. This takes a unique kind of courage and conviction.

Importantly, Curie was not convinced of the truth of this or that specific theory; rather, she placed her confidence in her own *ability to learn* and find out the truth, whatever that truth turned out to be. Can we have that same confidence and self-belief?

- Identify areas where you're holding back due to others' expectations, then take bold action that is aligned with your true capabilities. Your biggest breakthroughs often lie just beyond the edges of your comfort zone. Are you underestimating yourself? For example, if you've ruled out a certain course of study, career, lifestyle, or achievement as beyond you, pause and see if you might gently challenge yourself to expect more–even if nobody else holds that expectation of you.

- If you're feeling unconfident, think about all the achievements you've already made. In particular, think about how certain skills now seem easy to you, but when you first learned them, they were daunting and difficult. It's the same whenever we try something new. Try to remind yourself that it's always a little scary when you're doing something you've never done before. If you're starting a new job, meditate on how scary it was to learn to drive a car for the first time, and how you don't even think about it now. Tell yourself that with patience and hard work, what is difficult now can also be effortless in the future. Have faith in your ability to make that journey.

- Shift your focus from outcome to process. You cannot guarantee outcomes, but you can always show up to the work, keep your word, and apply with yourself with patient diligence. Have faith that whatever happens, you can live to your values and apply yourself to the fullest. There is comfort in that.

Share ideas before they're "perfect"

Curie actively shared her work with anyone interested in radiation, from physicists to doctors, leading to practical applications that saved lives. Some work environments can be highly competitive, and the science intelligentsia at the turn of the century certainly was. Unfortunately, this field tended to laud "great men" and lone geniuses who preferred their own intellectual heroism to group work and humble collaboration. But Marie was different, and her willingness to work with others–even when she hadn't figured everything out–was one of her greatest strengths.

Don't wait for your ideas to be perfectly polished; share them early to gather feedback and discover unexpected applications. True innovation happens at the intersection of different fields and perspectives.

- Don't fear feedback. In fact, actively seek it out. The faster you find out what you might be doing wrong, the sooner you can do it right. Rather than ignoring or arguing with someone's criticism of you, seek to find out if it has any basis, and if it does, ask them for more! Seek advice and welcome suggestions, even if it's not coming from the "right" places. A CEO may learn more about their market by chatting to random people in the street than by talking to their marketing experts and think tanks.

- Learn to be OK with never really being finished. It can be tempting to try to work away in secret isolation until we have some perfect, polished end result to show off proudly to others, but this is a risky strategy. We need the constant moderating influence of other minds. **Embrace the vulnerability of always *being in progress*.** Show people your first drafts, typos and all. Don't be afraid to let others see your trial and error. Speak your ambitions out loud even though you're not yet 100% clear on how you'll get there.

- Don't let vanity stop you from working with others. It's not a failure to share accolades. Nobel prizes, for example, are awarded as a recognition of "those who have conferred the greatest benefit to mankind" and are frequently shared between two or more people. What matters is the benefit to mankind, not the status of the one creating that benefit. Most of us can achieve more in collaboration than we can alone. Seek out a partner, a group, a feedback club, or simply get into the habit of considering other people's input on your work.

Mike's story

Mike had long believed that old piece of entrepreneurial wisdom: "Believe in yourself." And he certainly did believe in himself. He was a bold thinker, he was confident in his ideas, and he had no trouble speaking up about his vision, bravely trusting himself to fulfil it. And that was precisely the problem.

When Mike became obsessed with a new business idea, he embraced it with all his characteristic zeal and energy. He had built successful businesses from scratch before, and he would do it again. He was well-trained, experienced and hungry for success. He believed in himself.

So, when his young son began to weigh in and offer her advice and suggestions, he dismissed them without a second thought. Instead, he would make a "radical bet" on himself: he barged ahead in a totally different direction, made a staggeringly bad investment decision, and within 6 months had lost an embarrassing amount of money, not to mention made a flop of the new venture.

Even he had to admit it–his son had been right.

While boldness and self-belief are powerful, they need to be tempered with modesty, a spirit of collaboration, and enough humility to recognize when you are wrong. Mike's trouble was not his confidence, but *where* he placed that confidence. Because he saw himself as an expert, he mistakenly believed that every idea he had was automatically a good one. His son wasn't an expert like him, so what did he know? He dismissed his advice (along with anyone else's, for that matter), and paid the price.

"Nobel disease" is a tongue-in-cheek name for the tendency of some Nobel Prize winners to embrace bizarre and unscientific ideas, despite their expertise and intelligence. The idea is that, emboldened by their accolades, they lose perspective and fail to recognize when they are actually making cognitive errors. This phenomenon has also been called "The paradox of expertise". With growing knowledge can come a kind of narrow-mindedness and reluctance to accept good ideas and perspectives, especially if they come from others perceived as less qualified. Mike suffered from this phenomenon when he "believed in himself" to the point of not believing in anyone else.

He would have done well to take a page from Curie's book. She did not believe in *herself*, but in her process, in her work, and in the moderating power of humble collaboration with others. Marie Curie was literally a genius, but she knew that even she couldn't be right about everything!

Curie's high achiever mindset: "Real innovation is beyond fear, beyond conventions, beyond ego."

High achiever traits: Challenging conventions, collaboration with peers, self-conviction.

- Push against limits and boundaries placed on you by others, but don't argue your case. Instead, *show* that you can go beyond those limitations.
- When the world can't yet see or believe in your vision, take the risk and believe in yourself.
- Let go of the idealized, perfect outcome and get comfortable with the eternal process.

Questions for reflection:

What is one small risk that I can bravely take in my work right now?

Is there someone in my world I need to collaborate with?

In what ways can I be more vocal and visible in my goals and plans? How can I tell more people about what I'm doing even if I'm still "in progress"?

Herodotus

"That men do not learn very much from the lessons of history is the most important of all the lessons that history has to teach."

- **Aldous Huxley**

Our book so far has centered around an unspoken premise: By carefully considering the lives and works of notable historical figures, we in the present can *learn* something. We can extract the essence of these historical accounts and strategically apply them to our own lives, allowing us to achieve something of their success.

But have you ever considered that this very idea itself had to be invented?

Herodotus is known today as the "Father of History," precisely because he revolutionized how humanity understands its past. Not only did he himself live a life worth recounting and learning from, but he also gave humanity an entirely new way to look at other lives lived in the past.

History was never "invented" because, theoretically at least, it is merely an account of truth, albeit truth that happened long ago. But here is where things get a little meta: The study of history is a formal discipline with its own philosophical underpinnings and rules. One of the world's earliest inventors of that discipline was Herodotus.

Born in Halicarnassus (modern-day Turkey) to a wealthy merchant family, Herodotus spent his life traveling throughout the ancient world, meticulously documenting events, cultures, and stories that formed his masterwork "The Histories." In fact, it is from the name of this work that we get the English word "History." It derives from the Greek for "investigation."

The etymology is apt. Herodotus had a genuinely *systematic* approach to exploring and explaining historical events and brought factual documentation to life with his own observations, interpretations, and flair for storytelling. Herodotus happily wove together first-hand accounts, myth, personal observation, and pre-existing historical data to create a usable historical narrative, i.e., cause-and-effect accounts that were truly groundbreaking at the time.

Born around 485 BC, Herodotus' life predates anyone on this list. Though "recorded history" begins roughly when humanity invents writing, around 2600 BC, Herodotus' era heralded the invention of the historian as a kind of philosopher, whose work was to look back on these written records and construct from them a coherent narrative. Writers before Herodotus *had* kept records of isolated events, but it was Herodotus' genius that thought to compile a comprehensive and systematic collection of such stories that explain not just what happened, but why it happened, and what it might all mean, given the context.

Herodotus is credited with being the first to author a complete historical text (a record of the Greco-Persian Wars called "The Histories") and emphasize the need for an authoritative record–even if he himself wasn't quite what we'd consider an objective historian today. For example, his accounts were sometimes based on little more than secondhand eyewitness testimony, and included much embellishment and flat-out fantasy where he felt like it. This is undoubtedly why he has not just been called the Father of History, but also the "Father of Lies."

Not much is known about Herodotus on a personal level (early historians had yet to turn their attention to gathering information about the individual characters and personalities of history, after all!) but it is known that he travelled widely before settling in Athens. His curiosity took him all over the Middle East, and he explored Babylon and Syria, as well as Macedonia and parts of Eastern Europe.

On his travels, he spoke to people. He gathered up their oral accounts and memories like a natural scientist gathers samples and specimens. Encountering so many different people with so many different stories, he couldn't help but wonder how they all connected. What caused the Nile to flood? What was the actual lineage of the Greek gods, and who could remember such things? The big, eternal question was, *what came before now*, and how could we access it? Herodotus was a scientist and a philosopher, but his investigations concerned the nature and movement of time, and humanity's eternal dance within it.

Herodotus was incredibly methodical, recording everything he was told. Unfortunately, some of his accounts describe ants living in India that are bigger than foxes, men in Libya with faces in their chests and no heads, and sheep with tails so long they needed to be supported by little wheeled carts trailing behind them.

So, the question is, did Herodotus faithfully recount the tall tales and nonsense other people told him? Or are all these embellishments his own contribution? What matters, ultimately, is not what Herodotus recorded, but the fact that his recording in the first place was a rather novel innovation. Herodotus certainly got a lot wrong, and was widely criticized even in his own time for biased storytelling. But at the same time, his records, imperfect as they are, give us a peek into Ancient Greece and beyond, which we simply do not get from any other sources.

Herodotus, though a frequently unreliable narrator himself, was nevertheless very concerned with correcting misconceptions and accurately separating out myth from truth. "Very few things happen at the right time, and the rest do not happen at all. A conscientious historian will correct these defects," he says, amusingly. He claimed, for example, that his own research in Egypt revealed that Homer was mistaken in his epic poem about the Trojan War, and that really, Helen had never been kidnapped, but had been in Egypt the whole time.

While we can offer a little leeway to this early historian's first efforts, we can still appreciate the *spirit* in which Herodotus carried out his work, and the ultimate intention that drove him. He did not record mere dates and facts, but included rich details about architecture, customs, cultural and religious information, notes about fauna and flora, geographical details, weather, political organization, war and its machinery, and much more. Thanks to his records, we have some valuable insight into ancient life in Egypt, Assyria, and Persia.

Herodotus had a full life, and in 445 BC he was even granted a prize of 10 talents (around $200,000) in recognition of his contributions to Athenian society. He died around 425 BC when he was roughly 60 years old, and statues of his stylized likeness appear in university campuses and libraries all over the world.

In Herodotus' wake, the concept of historical analysis took root and became a valued part of intellectual life. It is hard to imagine what we would have of history today, 2500 years later, were it not for Herodotus' early efforts. Before Herodotus, there was only a motley assortment of local tradition and family memory; after him, the very spirit of history itself came alive, and he was said to have been inspired by the mythical Clio, the "Muse of History."

Herodotus's mode of questioning was systematic

Unlike previous writers who simply recorded disconnected tales, Herodotus developed his own comprehensive method of investigation. To compile his comprehensive travelogues, he conducted interviews, gathered evidence, made detailed observations and attempted to verify information through multiple sources.

This systematic approach meant that he didn't just document events and ideas, but strove to understand them. His work shows how organized documentation is sometimes the only thing that allows us to move from simple chronology to deep analytical investigation.

Herodotus blended entertaining storytelling with factual documentation

While his contemporaries focused solely on dry political accounts, Herodotus wove together grand historical events with cultural observations, local customs, and engaging narratives. Today, modern historians appreciate the value of documenting and studying the lives of "ordinary" people in everyday, non-military, non-politicized situations. Thus we have a history of everything–of mundane objects, of ideas, of fashion of all kinds, of social and cultural phenomena, of religion, even a history of history (for the interested, this is the field of *historiography*).

Herodotus' ability to balance entertainment with information enabled his work to survive and influence readers for millennia. Even when including questionable tales, he often qualified his accounts by noting their unverified nature, showing remarkable transparency about his methods. In his own way, Herodotus drew our attention to the eternal torment of the historian, namely, that to remember a story is often times to *invent* that story.

What are the limits of our own memories? How shall we take charge of the stories we tell about our own past? These big questions certainly haunted Herodotus, and they still haunt us today.

Document EVERYTHING like a master historian

Like Herodotus conducting his "autopsies" (personal inquiries), develop a systematic approach to gathering information. Today, the digital world is so thoroughly drenched with transient information that it can be hard to appreciate the need to stop and **write things down**. One consequence of this way of approaching information is that we become desperately *forgetful* as a species. We read something interesting, and a minute later, we instantly forget it again. The next distraction pops into awareness, the page scrolls down, and it's as though nothing ever happened.

Herodotus can teach us to stop and pay attention. Keep records. Take notes about what you're learning–the simple act of making a record tells your brain **"This is important, internalize this, remember this."** When you document well, you give your brain a chance to see bigger emergent patterns and themes. You start to develop a longer-range view. Your corresponding solutions become bigger and more sophisticated, too.

- Whether researching a project or exploring a new field, collect firsthand accounts, document observations, and verify through multiple sources. Track the data. Create your own "Histories" by maintaining detailed records not just of what happens, but why and how things occur. Try as much as you can to be neutral and objective. If you're trying a new gym program or work routine, for example, keep a journal where you monitor various metrics. The longer you keep these records, the richer your insights about the process will be.
- If something strikes you as interesting or relevant, don't let it get away! Record it so

you don't forget. You may find many interesting things to connect it to in the future. Plenty of research suggests that literally writing things down with pen and paper leads to better retention and recall than recording things digitally. Keep a series of notebooks close at hand wherever you go, or record voice notes on your phone to jot down later.

- Be organized. It doesn't matter what system of organization you use, only ensure that it works for you. Consider using the "Zetelkasten" (note box) system (essentially, your very own library or wiki system) or make use of color-coordinated notes and journals, summaries, mind maps, bullet lists, and so on. If you gather lots of data, you will likely need a tag or label system, so that you know what each piece of data is, where it belongs, and what it connects to.

Transform information into engaging stories

Herodotus opens his *Histories* saying this:

> "This is the display of the enquiry (*historiē*) of Herodotus the Halicarnassian–an enquiry made so that the things people have done don't get lost over time, and that the great and astounding actions of both Greeks

and barbarians (*barbaroi*) alike don't lose their glory (*kleos*). And especially it's an enquiry into the cause of why they went to war with each other."

Farther along, we reach Book 1, Section 5, which debates the supposed abduction of Helen of Troy. Take a look:

"(1) This is what the Persians say happened. And they trace the beginning of their hatred of the Greeks to the sack of Troy. (2) About Io, though, the Phoenicians do not agree with the Persians. For they say that they did not use force to carry her off to Egypt. Rather, she had sex with the captain of the ship while still in Argos. When she learned that she was pregnant, she was ashamed for her parents, and so she willingly sailed off with the Phoenicians before her shame became visible. (3) These are the things that the Persians and Phoenicians say. For my part, I'm not going to say whether these things happened in this or some other way. Rather, I'll identify and speak about the person who I know first wronged the Greeks, as I march on farther into my account, going through both small and great cities alike. (4) For those cities that were once great have now become small, while those that were great in my time were before small. Knowing that human happiness doesn't stay in the same place, I'll mention both alike."

As you can see, Herodotus didn't just list facts–he crafted narrative. The above is a complex weaving of actual record, personal interpretation, opinion, and bias, both acknowledged and unacknowledged. His intention was to present a picture of reality as it was in the past, more like an impressionist painter than a photographer. Though this somewhat undermined his reputation for factual truth, it also paradoxically makes his accounts more *memorable*.

- When sharing knowledge or presenting findings, weave in relevant cultural context and human elements. Of course, you shouldn't lie, but add some human color to make the truth come alive. *Tell stories.* If you're giving a presentation, for example, balance data with engaging anecdotes. By including emotion, motivation, and a little mystery, you present information in a way that is both informative and entertaining.
- Always be interested in causes and motivations. Data means nothing unless we embed it into a context that explains what came before that data, and what came after. Can you find cause-and-effect

relationships? For example, if you're trying to mediate a disagreement, try to paint a picture over time of how the current situation came to be for each party, one step at a time. A history of the conflict yields insights about its cause–which may give hints about how it can be resolved.

- Look for bigger themes. Every good story has a "moral." Can you connect even the most mundane and ordinary facts to something bigger and truer about life? Notice how Herodotus' account above ends with a rather philosophical musing about how "human happiness doesn't stay in the same place." Humans like stories because they point to things bigger than their immediate circumstances. You can make people connect with *your* story by doing the same.

Travel to deepen your understanding

Herodotus crossed the known world to gather firsthand knowledge–this was no easy feat at the time. While he was frequently criticized for basing his accounts on simple eyewitness testimony, the truth is that few of us have even that at the foundation of most of what we "know".

While it's common to call internet browsing "research," there is much more to gathering quality data than relying on Google and search algorithms. Take inspiration from Herodotus and go out into the world to get firsthand accounts from real people.

- While investigating any topic, go beyond second-hand sources. Visit locations, talk to people directly involved, and immerse yourself in the context. Whether researching a business opportunity or learning a new skill, seek direct experience rather than relying solely on others' accounts. Of course, literal travel may not always be an option, but try to be aware of the quality of your sources regardless. For example, instead of reading a social media post about an article about a politician's speech, find an unedited recording of that speech and watch/listen to it yourself.

- Sometimes, Herodotus himself was not sure what conclusion to come to regarding this or that historical event. But that's OK! Faithful historians always prefer an honest acknowledgment of the unknown over a satisfying but made-up explanation. If you're trying to understand some complicated political or cultural event in the past (or even in the present!) give yourself permission to simply gather data without necessarily rushing to a conclusion that isn't supported.

- When investigating the claims or stories of others, try as much as possible to contextualize them. You can learn a lot about a story if you know who told it, why they told it, and when and where they told it. Broadly, consider the origin of information and ideas. In Herodotus' account above, he tries to understand the hypothetical Helen's choices in terms of shame around an unintended pregnancy–a possible explanation both for her behavior and for subsequent storytellers to avoid recounting it accurately.

Tom's story

Tom is an intelligent, ambitious young man, but has the same persistent struggle as so many others just like him: an inability to focus. Despite being smart and driven, Tom constantly procrastinates and achieves well below what he knows is his potential. With every year that goes by, he feels as though he is falling further and further behind, and eventually, he knows something has to change, although he isn't sure what.

One day, while online, he come across something on social media: "10 little known signs of ADHD." Curious, he clicks on it and within an hour, he has gone down a rabbit hole and come out the other end, convinced that *this* has been his problem all along. He is hopeful. If this really is his problem, then he can fix it with the right medication and soon be able to quieten his mind and pay full, focused attention to the things that matter.

To his surprise, his friends and family are confused at this tentative self-diagnosis. And further to his surprise, Tom's doctor is not convinced either. Instead, he makes a suggestion: he tells Tom to keep a detailed record for six full months, closely tracking every lifestyle detail such as number of hours of sleep, time spent online, time spent exercising or outdoors, meals eaten, caffeine consumed, any physical illnesses, TV watched and so on. At the same time, he should monitor his overall ability to focus and concentrate.

Tom is annoyed and a little insulted, and seriously considers getting a second opinion, but he follows the doctor's suggestions. Fully intending to prove the doctor wrong, Tom goes out of his way to keep painfully detailed and specific notes of his every lifestyle choice.

When the six months are over, Tom sits down and looks at all these reams of data, and he cannot help but notice something: a curious week period where he rated his ability to concentrate as 10 out of 10 every single day. He never noticed this period before, and certainly didn't notice it at the time.

It was a week when he had gone to visit his girlfriend and work at her place instead. What did it all mean? After all, he'd had various visits of this length throughout the 6 months, and didn't report any better-than-normal concentration levels on those occasions. Then he remembered: that was the week that his girlfriend's internet was down. He had left his laptop at home and worked on other offline projects while there.

Tom didn't go back to the doctor. Instead, he raked through the data, this time looking for more clues. He kept gathering information, and by the end of ten months, he was certain of it: he did not have ADHD. Rather, he had certain bad habits that were consistently undermining his natural ability to focus and pay attention. These bad habits included drinking too much coffee, staying up late at night doom-scrolling on his phone, and going for days at a time without proper human interaction. When he reigned in these habits, he found that his ability to concentrate the following day was consistently greater.

Herodotus had certainly invented some fanciful stories in his time, but what Tom was learning was that **without plenty of well-organized, hard data, it was all too easy to resort to false explanations** and stories all the same. He had told himself a tale ("The reason I can't concentrate is because I have ADHD") but it simply wasn't true. Recording things properly revealed a truer, simpler story–one that he couldn't see without a broader, historical view. With proper records, he could construct a new narrative: "My attention tends to suffer if I make poor lifestyle choices."

It's an old adage that "those who cannot remember the past are doomed to repeat it," but this sentiment also applies to our own personal history, and our ability and willingness to learn from it. To be good historians of our own lives we need to respect what has gone before by documenting it and putting it to good use in the here and now.

Herodotus' high achiever mindset: "Through organized and well-documented stories about the past, I learn, and thus take control of my future."

High achiever traits: Thorough and comprehensive documentation, organization, data brought to life as narrative, travel, curiosity.

- Gather data about the past, stitch it together intelligently, and fashion for yourself a "history lesson" that gives you an advantage as you move into the future.

- To learn well, talk to everyone, listen carefully, and record everything.
- Don't be afraid of a little embellishment. Look at the data and see the *story* inside of it.

Questions for reflection:

Whether it's a question of my personal life or some specific project I'm working on, am I keeping accurate and usable records?

What is one thing I can do today to get a little more organized?

Being honest, have I relied a little too heavily on "second-hand sources," whatever that looks like in my life?

William Shakespeare

"Shakespeare teaches us more about being human than all the natural scientists combined."

- **Philip Kitcher**

Playwright William Shakespeare is not often included on lists such as ours, and for those who associated his name with boring high school English classes, he can seem irrelevant at best. But this 16th century poet, playwright, and actor certainly was a high achiever. He did not merely excel in his crafts, he completely revolutionized theatre, language, and the nature of storytelling itself. Author Harold Bloom begins his book, "Shakespeare: The Invention of the Human" like this:

The answer to the question "Why Shakespeare?" must be "Who else is there?"

While this may be overstating it a touch, there's no doubt that Shakespeare's contributions were unprecedented. While his contemporaries wrote stiff, formal works, Shakespeare created living characters so psychologically complex that they actually transformed how we understand human nature. When comparing his work to others of his time like Thomas Churchyard or George Whetstone, "a gulf in style, wit, richness, and ease of expression" separates their language from his. His achievement was extraordinary: His plays wove together multiple plot sources to create characters so alive that, 400 years later, they still shape how we understand ourselves–from young love (Romeo) to ambition (Macbeth) to intellectual doubt (Hamlet).

Like many of the great thinkers we explore in this book, Shakespeare's genius and his influence on the world is hard to appreciate precisely because we already live in a world so touched by his influence. Shakespeare not only coined more than 1700 new words, terms, and phrases (swagger, in a pickle, brave new world, cold-blooded, good riddance, green-eyed monster, "it's Greek to me") but he also crafted stories so rich and complex that humanity itself found a fitting symbolic vocabulary to tell its own story.

Shakespeare has been dead for more than 400 years, but really, he is everywhere in the modern world. His stories and characters are to this day echoed in operas, ballets, plays, movies, and TV series, his poems are read at funerals, and brides walk down the aisle to music composed by Mendelssohn for the wedding at the end of *A Midsummer Night's Dream*. Shakespeare pretty much invented the idea of "comic relief" during tense or tragic moments in a story, the idea of comedic mistaken identities, and the concept of "breaking the fourth wall." When you sit down to watch a movie or read a novel, much of what you expect to happen in the narrative comes from conventions that Shakespeare has deeply instilled in the Western mind.

There is a big difference between someone who is merely good at something, someone who is highly proficient at that thing, and someone who has so thoroughly mastered it that they permanently shift the entire endeavor to another dimension. To achieve excellently is a quantitative project, but to be the kind of high achiever that Shakespeare was, we need to make a qualitative leap and go far beyond the entire paradigm.

Shakespeare was not an academic or a virtuoso—he was primarily a storyteller, and his chosen and cherished theme was the human soul. His stories were not just entertainment (although they were most definitely that) they were creations that articulated something deeper and truer about life and the way we humans move through it.

As the Jungian psychologists and symbolic poets and theorists like to tell us, storytelling is about human psychology, and narratives are a unique way to discover who we are, to describe accurately what it feels like to be who we are, and to celebrate and mourn all that that entails. Whether through comedy or romance, weddings or wars, triumph or tragedy, Shakespeare points to the deepest fundamentals of the human experience–and, by giving us new language for those experiences, he even helped shape them.

Are you sitting comfortably? Here is a story for you: On the 26th of April 1564, on the feast day of Saint George, patron saint of England, a young boy named William Shakespeare was born in a half-timbered Tudor house on Henley Street. He was the third of eight children, his father was a successful glover and his mother a member of the landed gentry in their home village of Stratford-upon-Avon, a small market town of around 2000 people.

He attended grammar school and received a formal education in Latin, the classics, rhetoric, and the like, then graduated and married Anne Hathaway (she was 26 years old and he was 18; English law at the time considered him underage, so he had to apply for a special marriage license). He had three children, and managed a successful play company called the Lord Chamberlain's Men in London. He retired around 1613 and in 1616, he passed away of unknown causes on the same date as he had been born, at the age of 52 years old. The end.

But what happened during all that space in between? During Shakespeare's relatively short life, he produced around 38 plays, 154 sonnets, two long narrative poems and a handful of sundry poems and verses. Today, his works have been translated into over 100 languages, his plays have been brought to life on stages across the globe, and they have been performed more than the works of any other playwright.

But of the man himself, very little is known. All we have today is speculation, legend, and rumor about his appearance, his religious beliefs, his sexuality, his personality, and his work habits.

But we have his stories. While there has been much speculation about what is "true" about Shakespeare's history and biography, the man himself taught us that art, in its own strange way, is a kind of lie that tells us a bigger truth. By reading his works, we can not only appreciate the depth of Shakespeare's vision, but we see a glimpse of his own attitude and perspective, and see reflected in the speech of his characters some of his own questions, joys, and torments.

Between 1589 and 1613, Shakespeare created most of his notable works. His early plays were comedies and histories, and he later shifted to his famous tragedies–the most memorable being *Hamlet*, *Othello*, *King Lear*, and *Macbeth*. In his final years, he wrote a blend of both, and produced tragicomedies, often collaborating with other playwrights.

Shakespeare's story was a story about stories, and his life was lived in contemplation of life. But what can we learn from The Bard? Is the eternal high school student's accusation of "boring" and "irrelevant" true for us, or can Shakespeare teach us something about how to achieve excellence? Let's narrow things down a little.

Shakespeare possessed a unique ability to combine artistic genius with mass appeal

Unlike academic poets who wrote for elite audiences, Shakespeare created works of profound artistic sophistication that also reliably got "bums on seats." His works operated on multiple levels simultaneously: the groundlings got their bawdy jokes while nobles pondered the deeper philosophical questions. As Harold Bloom notes, "He thought more comprehensively and originally than any other writer," yet never at the expense of dramatic momentum.

The language of Shakespeare's time may give modern readers the mistaken impression that his works were overly formal and highbrow, the truth was that attending a Shakespeare play was like going to the cinema or watching a soap opera. In fact, not only was Shakespeare not boring, he took the dull stories of history and brought them to life on the stage–Cleopatra and Antony, King Richard the Second, Henry the Fifth, Macbeth–if they had a penny to pay for it, even the illiterate could enjoy the intrigues and exploits of history's most famous characters.

It's this consistent ability to blend "high" and "low" art that gives Shakespeare's work its unique timbre. This is not just a stylistic choice or something done out of necessity. Shakespeare's proficiency here is really proficiency in *communication*. He could appreciate that every person in his audience was coming to his play with a different set of expectations, and a different interpretive lens. Rather than this being a problem, however, it could be understood as something that forces one to look beyond superficial differences and "speak to the human condition" beneath them.

Without knowing it, many of us have very fixed ideas about what is sophisticated and what is not, what is current and what is outdated, what is fleeting or fashionable and what is fundamental. Shakespeare, however, had a mind broad enough to take in a reality that had room for *all* of this at once; the problems faced by Hamlet, for example, are eternal human struggles, and the high and the low can–and often do–change places.

In fact, the ancient Roman playwright, Publius Terentius, was the first to express this sentiment: *Homo sum, humani nihil a me alienum puto,* or "I am a human being, nothing human can be alien to me." High achievers are often able to break paradigmatic boundaries because they're so willing to break these smaller ones first: Who says that deep philosophy has to be difficult and boring? Who says that a serious tale about the human condition can't also be a fun night out? Who says you can't laugh during a tragic play or have an existential crisis during a comedy?

Shakespeare turned human complexity into an art form

Shakespeare did not try to force the complexity of human beings into his own rigid categories. He did not make sermons or lecture people. He did not bring the unfathomability of human life down to a more manageable level, but instead *rose* to meet the ambiguity, poignancy, and unpredictability of real human life.

Where other writers created flat characters representing single traits, Shakespeare invented psychologically complex beings that changed how we understand human nature itself. Before Shakespeare, it was not uncommon to have characters who were scarcely people at all, but rather allegorical, almost pantomimic, figures–a persona wearing black called "Death" would lurk in the background, for example, or "Vanity" would prance and preen in a comical wig.

In fact, Before Queen Elizabeth's reign, the only drama a person would likely encounter would be religious plays during local festivals, stuffy and unintelligible Greek and Roman productions for university students, or vanity projects funded by wealthy nobles for peasants. These plays were closer in tone and structure to church services than anything that we would recognize as true theatre.

Shakespeare's genius lay in weaving together countless influences–from ancient texts to local gossip, from court politics to kitchen tales–into stories that revealed fundamental truths about being human. He didn't just write great speeches; he created living minds on stage that still feel more real than most actual historical figures. Bringing complexity and psychology to theatre, then, was a little like switching from black and white to color or, more accurately, from two dimensions to three. How can we bring this kind of qualitative leap into our own lives?

Master the art of "Substantive Nonsense"

Stephen Booth is a Shakespeare scholar who focuses on the *poetics* of Shakespeare's language–how it operates on audiences–rather than traditional interpretation or biographical/political contexts. Booth argues that Shakespeare's genius lies in creating rich, multilayered networks of phonetic, semantic, and ideational patterns that work *below* the threshold of conscious attention. Subtle linguistic choices can influence an audience's experience and moral alignment; thus Shakespeare's genius was not just about the words he put on paper, but the *experience* created through language, often in ways not consciously recognized.

"Substantive nonsense" points to a kind of playfulness and limberness when working on multiple levels simultaneously. Rather than waste too much time trying to be clever on the most obvious level, build *layers* into your projects that reward different levels of engagement. The deepest impact often comes from patterns that audiences feel without consciously noticing.

- If you're trying to be creative and innovative, give yourself permission to stop trying so hard, and *explore in another dimension entirely.* You may be repeatedly hitting a wall trying to come up with some clever new candy flavor ideas, but what if you didn't need a new flavor at all? What if you played around with ways that the customer themselves could customize their own chocolate? Or what if you began selling mystery packs of unknown chocolate? You're suddenly working on an entirely different level; you're no longer just selling candy flavors, you're selling intrigue and surprise.
- When looking for new patterns, links, connections, or layers, realize that you can't force it by being too systematic. Instead, disengage your rational, conscious mind and give your creative free-flowing unconscious mind a chance to toss out new ideas. Go for a walk, take a nap, throw yourself into a tough workout or do a completely unrelated task. When you

return, you may be able to see more clearly "outside the box."

- If you're feeling stuck, try turning your dilemma into a story. Play and have fun with it. What might your problem look like to an alien from outer space? How might you explain your problem to a child? How has a fairytale character solved this kind of dilemma in the past? This sort of thing may seem silly in the moment, but it can yield powerful results!

- What are you currently assuming is 100% true about your situation? Play around with *inverting* it. What if, instead of trying to find ways to get customers to come to you, you visited *them* in their homes? Put on fresh eyes and be willing to question what seems unquestionable.

Turn your time crunch into a superpower

Shakespeare wrote Macbeth because his company needed a new play, fast. He was running a business, facing deadlines, and keeping actors employed, and he used this pressure to create timeless art. Next time you're overwhelmed with deadlines, think like Shakespeare: Instead of just surviving the crunch, use it to force innovative solutions. Can't perfect every detail? Good. Work fast, combine unexpected ideas, and trust that constraints often create more interesting results than perfect conditions.

- Are you dawdling and procrastinating? Stuck in analysis paralysis? One way to break free is to give yourself less time to complete the task, not more. Sit down, set the timer, and get to work like your life depends on it. Don't stop to second guess or make excuses.
- Try not to get too attached to how you think a problem *should* be solved, or the form you think an innovation *should* take. If you don't get too hung up on format, then you open yourself up to so many more options and possibilities. For example, if something just isn't working verbally, why not experiment with expressing it non-verbally? In the same way as Shakespeare's written words come to life when performed in real time by flesh-and-blood human beings, see what your message looks like when expressed on a totally different wavelength. Not only will you see things from a different perspective, but you'll also probably save yourself time and effort.
- Deliberately do things wrong. It sounds counterintuitive, but trying on purpose to fail or deliberately conjuring up the wrong solutions can paradoxically take you to

where you want to be. Sometimes, being too fearful of making a mistake can kill momentum and keep us stuck. Instead, *make those mistakes* and see where you land. If, for example, you're struggling to correctly form a certain calligraphy letter, try to first exaggerate the error you're making. This makes the correct path so much more obvious–the right way will be precisely the opposite.

Make everything feel like real life, even when it's not

Shakespeare didn't write characters, he *created people*. And people don't always follow formulas. Abandon the idea of perfection, completeness, or easy comprehensibility. Real life is more nuanced than this, and if you can take an approach that *accommodates* this nuance, you instantly create a feeling of more depth and authenticity.

- If you're designing an app or leading a team, stop thinking about features or functions and start thinking about human psychology. Why does Hamlet's hesitation feel so familiar? Because Shakespeare understood how humans actually work, not just how they're *supposed* to work. Study your audience or the people you're working with like Shakespeare studied his–not just their obvious needs, but their secret doubts, unspoken hopes, and inner contradictions. This is how you can better connect with them.

- Add in a small amount of the unexpected. Chocolatiers know that a little salt or even chili can make chocolate seem sweeter and richer, and perfumers know that a tiny amount of a "bad" smell in a formula is somehow more beautiful and compelling than a blend of uninteresting albeit pretty scents. In your own work, leave a few things ambiguous, unfinished, or even a little controversial. Don't be too neat. Leave room for mystery and strangeness.

- Be playful. There is often a great deal of truth, value, and beauty in humor and absurdity. In Shakespeare's plays, misunderstandings, struggles, and conflicts are not a problem to solve but rather part of the enjoyment and mystery of life itself. If you're struggling with a problem, can you shift perspective and see the value in the problem just as it is? Can you showcase the unusual, the imperfect, the vulnerable, the strange, the incomplete–i.e., the *human*? For example, instead of spending money to "renovate" a quirky historic building for your restaurant, make the quirkiness part of the dining experience, and play it up.

Ray's story

Ray was a smart man. A *really* smart man. He had a political science PhD from Harvard, a handful of degrees from the London School of Economics, and a devastating knack for language. He was an astute and original thinker, and by his early twenties he was already in possession of a sophisticated and unique life philosophy that earned him genuine respect in his field. So he did what any successful academic does at the height of their career: He set his mind to *sharing* this worldview.

Ray knew his field inside and out, and in debate he could trump anyone, whether they were ideological opponents or his own peers. He was intelligent, enthusiastic, and at the top of his game. The world was his oyster, right? Not quite.

On the evening of a book launch for a new work he had published, he realized with disappointment that the only people who attended were other academics in his small, niche field. His friends and family were ultra-proud of him, of course, but they had very little understanding of what he actually *did*, and their eyes invariably glossed over when he tried to explain his latest big idea, or just how important his newest publication was.

Eventually, Ray had something of a crisis of confidence, and lost faith in himself. What was he even doing, anyway? Did it matter? Did people think that his work was boring? A concerned friend hauled him off one evening to a stand-up comedy night to take his mind off things. Ray grumbled and complained, but it was a night that would change the course of his life.

The main act was a clever and quick-witted comic who delivered a full 45-minute set without breaking a sweat. He had every single person in the audience eating out of his hand, and Ray was astonished at how they listened with rapt attention, laughed, clapped, listened again. What really astonished Ray, however, was the *content* of the comic's routine: he was making outrageously funny observations about all the same topics and themes that Ray himself was an expert on. And yet this audience was not bored in the least. They *got* it.

That night Ray couldn't sleep. In the morning, he made a rash decision: He'd learn to do standup. Nobody could understand why, and they tried to discourage him; wasn't comedy a little... low brow? Wasn't it a shame to let a great mind like his go to waste on being, well, an entertainer? But Ray had had a vision that night: The comedian had understood something he didn't, and he wanted desperately to learn.

Over the course of the next few years, Ray threw himself into his new project with a fervor bordering on mania, and he made rapid advances. Stand-up comedy was a lot harder than it looked, but he was driven by a deep hunger to speak his mind, to share all his big ideas that had, until now, been stagnating in dull academic papers and half empty conference halls.

To everyone's astonishment, Ray was pretty good, and it was precisely because of the insights he could bring from his background. He studied the masters–but this time it was not the great political and philosophical masters, but the legendary comedians who arguably knew more about the human condition, communication, rhetoric, and creativity.

Over time, Ray gained more confidence and a reputation for smart and surprising humor that seemed to attract people from all walks of life. Ray had learned that a good speech, a well written essay, or a thoroughly logical argument could only get you so far. If he really wanted people to *listen*, in their hearts and in their souls, he would need to speak a higher, more complex language. His jokes were playful, lyrical, and completely unexpected. They made people laugh *and* they made people think.

He had once thought that the most intellectually challenging thing a human could do was to excel in some prestigious scholarly field. Now he knew that the magic lies somewhere *between* and *beyond* those fields. He understood economics and politics better when he injected it with a little of the humor and absurdity of the human condition, and he understood comedy better when he applied to it all the deepest insights from Locke, Hobbes, and Rousseau.

Ray had been a high achieving academic. But he became a *groundbreaking* comedian. His jokes were layered, and his specialty was the ambiguous pun and "lexical ambiguity" (two jokes in one, depending on the political assumptions of the listener). By playing with the superficial this way, he learned to speak to deeper human fears and yearnings–and his audience loved the experience. He could even make people laugh with nothing more than a perfectly timed eyebrow lift. Instead of writing lengthy tomes on this or that complex bit of theory, he discovered he could make people *get it* with a single well-crafted joke.

Shakespeare's high achiever mindset: "Creativity doesn't wait for the perfect moment. It fashions its own perfect moments out of ordinary ones."

High achiever traits: Playfulness, creatively blending "high" and "low", out-of-the-box thinking, embracing the human.

- Engaging with human complexity is an art form. Work with real life as you find it, rather than trying to limit its strangeness to fit your mental model.
- Be curious and make no assumptions about where fresh ideas and solutions may come from.
- Creativity and novelty are *everywhere*. Find eternity in a tight deadline, heroism in the mundane, and profundity in the everyday. Be willing to see things with fresh eyes.

Questions for reflection:

Am I unnecessarily limiting myself?

In what ways might my current problem/challenge actually be a source of fresh inspiration?

Might my own idea about what a solution *should* look like be getting in the way of me actually finding a solution?

Mozart

"The music is not in the notes, but in the stillness between them."

- **Mozart**

Mozart (full name Joannes Chrysostomus Wolfgangus Theophilus Mozart) was a musical prodigy who revolutionized classical music in his tragically short 35-year life. Born in 1756 to an established and well-respected family of professional musicians in Salzburg, in the Holy Roman Empire (now Austria). Mozart was composing masterpieces by age seven and soon became one of the most prolific and influential composers in Western musical history. Today he is frequently considered one of the world's first "child prodigies" and his unique flavor of genius has never quite been repeated.

Despite facing financial struggles and personal challenges throughout his life, Mozart created hundreds of works that transformed musical expression, bridging the Classical and Romantic eras with his extraordinary technical genius and emotional depth.

Mozart was a totally unique individual, and he had a totally unusual life. He was the last of seven children, five of whom did not live past infancy. He was tutored almost from infancy by his father Leopold, along with two other siblings, in particular his older sister Marie-Anna, a brilliant musician in her own right. Marie-Anna recounts how the three-year-old Mozart would watch in interest as their father tutored her in piano:

> *"He often spent much time at the clavier (piano), picking out thirds, which he was ever striking, and his pleasure showed that it sounded good... In the fourth year of his age his father, for a game as it were, began to teach him a few minuets and pieces at the clavier... He could play it faultlessly and with the greatest delicacy, and keeping exactly in time... At the age of five, he was already composing little pieces, which he played to his father who wrote them down."*

Marie-Anna, who some believe was as talented as Mozart or even more so, was forced to give up performing after her marriage, and sadly nothing of her work survives today. Mozart did not have a childhood as such, but spent his early years travelling Europe and giving concerts. In the 18th century, travel of this kind was arduous, and the precocious Mozart was already dissatisfied with the limits of what he was being taught, and the heavy expectations placed on him by his father.

From almost the moment he was born, Mozart was given a heavy burden. He grew up in a house filled with music and as a toddler dabbled with instruments before he could do almost anything else. By the impossibly tender age of five he could play piano and violin proficiently, and by seven he was giving performances to European royalty, performing a European grand tour before he was a teenager. Even from a young age his piano and violin performances were virtuosic, and by 11 years old his compositions were being commissioned by the Austrian nobility and artistic elite, and he was performing in royal courts and winning praise.

At 17 he was already a successful and fully developed professional musician, and turned his eye to composition, writing many concertos, operas, symphonies, and more. Throughout his life he would have a complicated relationship with music, with fame, and with money, and though he was a glittering virtuoso who had enjoyed easy and ample fame, he often struggled financially.

He has been described as a thin man of slight stature, with intense eyes and a small voice. He was intelligent and erudite, and known for his love of fine dress and elegant surroundings. He would grace the stage in gold and crimson, with a stark white formal wig and other finery. This is perhaps an image difficult to reconcile with Mozart's other characteristics, namely a taste for the vulgar (the biographies kindly refer to his "scatological humor"), and a predilection for practical jokes.

Fluent in many languages, he was fond of witty and crude word play, and liked billiards, dancing, and socializing. He wrote filthy letters to his own cousin and composed rude mock canons. His widowed wife changed the words of his canon "Leck mich im Arsch" (euphemistically, "kiss my ass") to "Lasst froh uns sein" ("let us be glad") before agreeing to publish it. Considering Mozart's non-existent childhood, we can see this playful and childish rebellion in a gentler light, although some historians and biographers wondered if he actually suffered from Tourette's syndrome.

He had had a tumultuous and difficult relationship with his wife Constanze Weber, a soprano from Germany, and the couple had six children, although, in an echo of Mozart's own history, only two of these survived to adulthood. The two married when he was 26 years old under somewhat scandalous circumstances. He said of her, "It is, of course, a money marriage, nothing more. I wouldn't want to enter into this kind of marriage. I wish to make my wife happy and not make my happiness through her." At just 35 years old, he died under unclear circumstances, and had a modest funeral. To this day, the location of his remains is unknown.

In his short lifetime he created more than 800 works, many of which are adored today as much as they were back then. It would take a whopping 202 hours or almost 9 full days to listen to Mozart's complete body of work. Mozart wrote with ease in every genre and happily played many different types of instruments, but he is considered a particularly fine example of music of the Classical style–finely proportioned, and with a transparency and clarity that can clearly be seen in subsequent great composers who bore his influence.

Mozart possessed an unparalleled ability to transform discipline into creativity

His daily routine was packed full. In a 1777 letter to his father, we get a peek into his daily habits. The then 21-year-old Mozart describes his routine in Mannheim during a time he was actively looking for other employment:

> *"I am writing this at eleven at night, because I have no other leisure time. We cannot very well rise before eight o'clock, for in our rooms (on the ground-floor) it is not light till half-past eight. I then dress quickly; at ten o'clock I sit down to compose till twelve or half-past twelve, when I go to Wendling's, where I generally write till half-past one; we then dine. At three o'clock I go to the Mainzer Hof (an hotel) to a Dutch officer, to give him lessons in galanterie playing and thorough bass, for which, if I mistake not, he gives me four ducats for twelve lessons. At four o'clock I go home to teach the daughter of the house. We never begin till half past four, as we wait for lights. At six o'clock I go to Cannabich's to instruct Madlle. Rose. I stay to supper there, when we converse and sometimes play; I then invariably take a book out of my pocket and read..."*

If you think that sounds busy, consider a letter he wrote in 1782, five years later, after his career had grown substantially:

"At six o'clock in the morning I have my hair dressed, and have finished my toilet by seven o'clock. I write till nine. From nine to one I give lessons. I then dine, unless I am invited out, when dinner is usually at two o'clock, sometimes at three, as it was to-day, and will be to-morrow at Countess Zichi's and Countess Thun's. I cannot begin to work before five or six o'clock in the evening, and I am often prevented doing so by some concert; otherwise I write till nine o'clock [...] At half-past ten or eleven I go home, but this depends on the mother's humor, or on my patience in bearing it. Owing to the number of concerts, and also the uncertainty whether I may not be summoned to one place or another, I cannot rely on my evening writing, so it is my custom (especially when I come home early) to write for a time before going to bed. I often sit up writing till one, and rise again at six."

For those keeping track, that's roughly 5 hours of sleep. And yet, Mozart was frequently referred to as having a humorous, charming, and light disposition, and though he worked tirelessly, he found ample time for recreation and socializing. Many biographers have since painted a picture of a kind of *disciplined chaos.*

His daily routines revealed a remarkable blend of structured productivity and artistic spontaneity. His ability to create complex, emotionally rich compositions while maintaining an incredibly disciplined work ethic set him apart from his contemporaries.

Mozart's musical genius was to find joy and humor in art

Unlike many serious composers of his time, Mozart infused his music with a sense of playful brilliance. He would sign letters backwards, write musical jokes that poked fun at inferior musicians, and approach composition with a childlike sense of wonder. This ability to blend technical mastery with emotional spontaneity allowed him to create music that was both intellectually sophisticated and emotionally accessible.

He explained, "Neither a lofty degree of intelligence nor imagination nor both together go to the making of genius. Love, love, love, that is the soul of genius."

So what is this love he is talking about?

"When I am... completely myself, entirely alone... or during the night when I cannot sleep, it is on such occasions that my ideas flow best and most abundantly. Whence and how these ideas come I know not nor can I force them."

We can work hard, structure our lives with faithful discipline, and continuously press ourselves to the very limits of our abilities... but at some point, we need to pause and find those silent spaces *between* the notes, those quiet moments where ideas flow into our minds, those thoughts that we know not from whence they come.

Creativity of all kinds–not just music or art or literature–requires a careful combination of two seemingly unrelated skills: the ability to throw oneself into hard work, and the ability to laugh, play, be silly, and relish with joy the new ideas that spring to mind.

Design a routine that fuels your creativity

Like Mozart, who carved out specific times for composition despite a packed schedule, create a daily framework that protects your most creative hours. Mozart would sometimes only get a chance to work on his own compositions late into the night, after he had fulfilled all his other obligations. But he still did it!

- If you're a writer, artist, or entrepreneur, identify your peak productivity times and guard them fiercely. Don't just hope inspiration strikes—schedule it. Set aside uninterrupted blocks for your most important work, treating them as sacred appointments with your potential. Rather than trying to work on important projects last thing at night, with whatever time and energy you have left over from other things, schedule these tasks for when you're at your best wherever possible.

- Try to cultivate your own "disciplined chaos." It may take time to find your own flow, but recognize that there is plenty of time in a day if you use it well. Listen to audio books on your commute, mull over important problems while at the grocery store, or rehearse lines or routines in your imagination when you're doing everyday chores.

- Make use of creative task-switching. While it may be fatiguing to give lessons for five hours in a row, say, you may actually get more done if you mix things up. Squeeze in routine tasks around the edges of bigger and more challenging ones, or piggyback difficult projects on easy and more automatic ones. Many composers explain how their best creative moments come to them not during "work hours" but in the spaces between, i.e. when they're out working, having dinner with friends, or brushing their teeth. Stay flexible, and keep moving.

- At the end of every day, pause deliberately. Even if it's just for five minutes, take the time to just process what has occurred that day. Be quiet. Let ideas come.

Inject playfulness into serious work

Mozart never lost his sense of humor, even in his most complex compositions. He was known to be constantly wise-cracking and telling jokes ("What's even worse than a flute? Two flutes!") and would undertake even difficult and grueling work with a sense of levity and whimsy.

Mozart once bought a starling, and when the bird died he gave it a full funeral, wrote a poem in its honor, and erected a tombstone in his garden. He is reported to have taught the bird to sing a melody he composed, although he claimed that, despite being an excellent musician, the starling had sung a G# instead of G in one part, and incorrectly extended a note in another.

While this is all in good fun, the truth is that all this was happening during a rather melancholy and difficult time in Mozart's life. His father, with whom he had always had a complicated relationship, had passed away. A close friend had also died, and he was working on *Don Giovanni*, a comedic opera that nevertheless has some rather dark themes and undertones.

The point is that through it all, Mozart was able to introduce a little lightness and absurdity. He composed a piece designed to poke fun at bad musicians, with passages played deliberately out of tune ("a musical joke") and despite his love for haute couture and luxury hairpieces, he was not above a fart joke. "Whoever is most impertinent" he claimed, "has the best chance."

- Find ways to make your work enjoyable, not just for yourself but for those experiencing it. Many of us deliberately downplay the weird, childish, or silly parts of our personalities, when these parts are in fact our most endearing and unique. Whether you're giving a presentation, developing a product, or solving a complex problem, look for moments of unexpected delight. **Creativity is closely connected with play**; deliberately see the strange or absurd in the everyday. See things as a child would. Making people laugh and creating something great are not mutually exclusive!
- There is a fine line between comedy and tragedy. You can cut tension, create relief, and increase your own feeling of resilience by learning to laugh a little at life's

torments. A well-timed joke can get things moving, or smooth over awkwardness or a misunderstanding. As they say, the show must go on! But we can always laugh at ourselves, and choose not to take it all too seriously.

- Amuse yourself. Mozart would frequently give saucy or outrageous titles to works in progress before they were polished and sent off to royalty. Just because you are working hard on a serious problem doesn't mean you can't have some fun with it. Instigate a little banter, play a light-hearted prank, or poke a little fun at what's supposed to be somber and serious. Play with colorful or unexpected language, be silly, or ask a bold and unexpected question. Make bad puns. Dare to be a little sassy. Humor is one of humanity's greatest stress management tools, after all, and there's no rule that says that genius has to be boring.

Master the art of white space thinking

Mozart's genius wasn't just in the notes he wrote, but in the spaces between them. His ability to compose complex musical works often emerged from periods that seemed unproductive. In his letters, he sometimes describes moments of seemingly idle time— reading a book after supper, conversing with friends, or spending time with Constanze—that were actually critical to his creative process.

These "white spaces" were where his musical ideas gestated. Unlike many artists who equate productivity with constant work, Mozart understood that creativity requires periods of apparent stillness. "Believe me," he says, "I do not like idleness, but work." However, we can reframe things so that "work" is a much-varied activity that includes both tension and release, effort and recoil, active expression and passive contemplation. **Perfectly timed rest, then, enables work in the same way that silence enables music.**

- Cultivate your own white space thinking by allowing yourself moments of apparent unproductivity. Take walks, engage in meandering conversations, read widely, and trust that these seemingly empty moments are actually when your most innovative ideas are taking shape.
- Know when to just stop. Forcing yourself to work when you're depleted will only yield diminishing returns, damage your mood, and create a feeling of resentment and struggle. Instead, find *rhythm* in your workflow; your breaks will be sweeter if they follow sincere and intense work, and your work will be richer if it follows

periods of peace and restoration. Importantly, try to truly rest, rather than go through the motions while you're anxiously thinking about all the things you should be doing. Even geniuses need to go on vacation or play a game of billiards sometimes.

- If you have a serious problem or a truly challenging ordeal you're trying to manage, realize that you can always set your burden aside for a time. Mozart was financially supporting his family as a 10-year-old, yet he did what he needed to do without becoming bitter or discouraged. His father was overbearing and difficult to please, but Mozart strove for a sense of independence and happiness anyway. Despite much adversity in life, Mozart found time for cheerfulness, joy, and good humor. When told that *Don Giovanni* contained some "lovely music, even better than Figaro, but not meat for the teeth of the Viennese," Mozart retorted "Give them more time to chew it." We can take the same approach to events in our own lives. Be patient. Give yourself time to chew things over.

Lily's story

In her time as a team leader for a massive global corporation, Lily had already overseen countless negotiations. However, when she was roped in to help with an important acquisition, she found herself in new territory altogether.

After months of strategic discussions and meetings, all the financial evaluations had been done, all the legal due diligence had been completed, and all the operational considerations thoroughly analyzed. However, there was still one spanner in the works: Many parties were finding it tough to agree on the timeline for the integration plan. The new company had a noticeably different work culture, and it was becoming clear that their long-term vision and objectives were quite different from the bigger company's.

The meetings and discussions drew on, and became steadily more desperate. One party felt rushed, the other felt needlessly held up. They brought in mediation experts and lawyers and other experts, each weighing in on the problem with their own earnest theories, agendas, and protocols.

Lily, being the chief business analyst of her team, was feeling the pressure to resolve the situation, or else lose the deal entirely. One day, after a grueling meeting with all the usual bigwigs, she stepped outside and encountered the COO in the break room. Big black bags under his eyes, he looked utterly exhausted and defeated. Without thinking, Lily approached and cracked a joke, playfully suggesting that he looked like hell, and did he need a drink?

He stared at her. It was a totally brazen thing to say, and for a moment Lily wondered if she had blown it. But to her surprise, the COO burst out laughing. "A drink? Don't know if that will be enough... what else have you got?" he groaned.

Lily laughed in relief and then had a flash of insight. "You know what always makes me feel better? *Tacos*. And I know just the place."

Again he stared at her, taken aback. However, within an hour, Lily had convinced the entire delegation to abandon their stuffy meeting room, kick off their uncomfortable formal shoes and make their way to the local taco joint. To the outside observer, the idea seemed preposterous: A dozen professionals in suits crowding into a tiny mom and pop Mexican joint. They had all been butting heads for months, yet somehow, as the night wore on and everyone ate and relaxed, tensions melted.

The tequila flowed. Nobody mentioned the merger, but as the group laughed and talked, everyone relaxed and let their guard down. Soon, the feeling was mutual: Wasn't all this stress about the timeline a little *silly*?

In the morning, all parties were severely hungover and a little sheepish, but by the end of the week the final stages of the merger were completed. Concessions were made, adjusted timelines were agreed upon and people were feeling generous and conciliatory.

Though it was never officially acknowledged, everyone knew that the big shift had come that night Lily had dragged everyone away from the boardroom for the evening. Though any business expert would have considered it madness to act so unprofessionally, the truth was that a little spontaneity and fun was precisely what was needed. The evening was playful, light. It may have been a little messy, but it was *human*.

Mozart's high achiever mindset: "The supreme accomplishment is to blur the lines between work and play."

High achiever traits: Disciplined chaos, productive rest, "white space" thinking, balanced routines.

- Create a daily schedule that supports not just consistent hard work, but time for restful regeneration, play, and spontaneous creativity.
- Don't take anything–especially yourself–too seriously.

- "Spontaneous" creative insight will usually come to those who have been working hard!

Questions for reflection:

Classical music is characterized by balance and symmetry, harmony, dynamic range and contrast, and well-proportioned variation in all its sounds, textures, and harmonies. Look at your own daily schedule and routine as though it were a composition by Mozart, and ask yourself:

Do I have enough rest, white space, and room to breathe in my schedule? Is that white space balanced and well-distributed throughout my day?

Have I included enough space for playfulness, levity, creativity, spontaneity, and even absurdity in my day-to-day routine?

If my life is a melody, what currently strikes me as "out of tune" or unharmonious, and how can I go about making things smoother and more comfortable?

Printed in Dunstable, United Kingdom